Modaris and Diamino for Apparel Design

Modaris and Diamino

for Apparel Design

Catherine Black

Florida State University

Fairchild Books, Inc.

New York

Director of Sales and Acquisitions: Dana Meltzer-Berkowitz

Executive Editor: Olga T. Kontzias

Senior Development Editor: Jennifer Crane

Development Editor: Michelle Levy

Art Director: Adam B. Bohannon

Production Manager: Ginger Hillman

Senior Production Editor: Elizabeth Marotta

Copyeditor: Joanne Slike

Cover Design: Kristina O'Toole

Cover Art: Corbis

Text Design: Mary Neal Meador

The content of this Book only engages its authors; Lectra SA and
any of the companies of the Lectra Group are not responsible
whatsoever for the contents of this book or any representation
made therein. The Modaris and Diamino software are copyright-
ed by Lectra and proprietary to Lectra and only Lectra can grant
the required licenses for the use of this software. Any use of the
Modaris or Diamino software without the appropriate licenses
granted by Lectra is unlawful.

Library of Congress Catalog Card Number: 2006940799

ISBN: 978-1-56367-466-2

GST R 133004424

Printed in the United States of America

TP13

Contents

Extended Contents

Extended Contents

Preface

Why Lectra?

An understanding of computer-aided design (CAD) is essential for apparel design students, as well as industry professionals. The importance of computer knowledge cannot be ignored; for future designers, hands-on skills with CAD programs are essential.

Lectra is a world leader, providing a comprehensive range of software and hardware dedicated to industrial users of textiles, leather, and other soft materials. With more than 17,000 customers in more than 100 countries, Lectra brings technology to the apparel industry.

Why Modaris and Diamino?

The software chosen as the focus for this textbook are Lectra's Modaris and Diamino. Modaris is used for all phases of pattern development, including pattern manipulation, drafting, and grading. Pattern manipulation, drafting, and grading on the computer are accurate and efficient. After the patterns are created and graded, they are sent to Diamino, the marker-making program. Marker making is also accurate and efficient on the computer. This book provides instruction for students and professionals engaged in continuing education.

This book is designed for the novice or experienced user of Modaris and Diamino. It is intended as a guide to learning the Modaris and Diamino commands. The textbook demonstrates commands related to pattern making, pattern grading, and marker making. Each chapter includes definitions and an explanation of the commands used in the chapter. Hands-on application is provided through step-by-step exercises. The CD-ROM contains files that provide a starting point for many of the learning activities. The approach reinforces many of the same pattern manipulations found in flat-pattern books. The CD-ROM also features the art from the text in color.

Key terms that you need to be familiar with as a professional appear in bold type. To further enhance students' education, appendices with detailed descriptions of the commands and a glossary are included. At the end of each chapter, new terms and commands are highlighted. The goal is to stimulate technical and creative design students to create patterns and markers on the computer.

Modaris version 5.1 and Diamino version 5 are the basis for instructions in the book. This book can also be used with older versions of Modaris and Diamino. Modaris allows the creation of original patterns on-screen or from existing patterns provided on the CD-ROM. Diamino markers can also be produced on-screen or from existing markers provided on the CD-ROM. This makes the introduction of Modaris and Diamino application accessible to students of all levels.

Chapters 1 and 2 introduce Modaris. Readers familiar with computers will find similarities between the Modaris program and previous programs they have used. Chapter 3 covers the concept of digitizing. This chapter covers the inputting of basic pattern blocks, or slopers, into the computer. Chapters 4 through 6 cover pattern manipulation, pattern drafting, and completion of patterns. Pattern grading is covered in Chapter 7. Pattern grading is the process of increasing and decreasing the basic pattern size into a range of sizes. Chapter 8 contains information to produce a variant. A variant contains information similar to a cutter's must. Diamino is covered in Chapter 9.

What This Book Is Not

This book will teach you how to use the computer pattern-making program. It is not intended as a fundamental pattern-making, pattern-grading, and marker-making book. It is beyond the scope of this book to cover every tool that may be applied in production or applied to every pattern manipulation. Therefore, knowledge of pattern making and pattern grading are prerequisite. For further explanation of flat-pattern techniques and pattern-grading techniques, please refer to pattern-making and pattern-grading textbooks. Suggested books are listed in the References section.

Acknowledgments

It is always impossible to mention all the students and professional friends who have contributed by sharing their ideas with me, helping to make this book possible through their encouragement. My sincere thanks to the computer design students at Florida State University, who inspire me and continually challenge me each semester. I am especially indebted to Christiahna Douglass-Barnes and Kathryn Dawe, who worked tirelessly to review each exercise in the book. To the graduate students who have helped develop and teach computer design, Charles Freeman and Diana Sindicich, my special thanks. Lectra's Modaris and Diamino hold so much potential because of the people at Lectra who bring new dimensions to the study of computer design.

I consider Rinn Cloud, the former Department Chair of Textiles and Consumer Sciences at Florida State University, to be my professional mentor; thank you for your encouragement and support. Without your advice and friendship, I could not have undertaken or completed this project!

To everyone at Fairchild Books, thank you for the continuing support and encouragement throughout the process. Each of the following individuals should be recognized for their faith and contributions: Olga Kontzias, executive editor; Jennifer Crane, senior development editor; Michelle Levy, development editor; Elizabeth Marotta, senior production editor; Ginger Hillman, production manager; and Adam Bohannon, director of creative services and production, for the wonderful art direction. I am especially appreciative of all the work Michelle Levy spent on the development of this project—most especially setting deadlines and keeping me on track.

To the colleagues who spent time reviewing drafts, know that your contributions add so much in the development of the end product: Andrew Burnstine, Jean K. Dilworth, and Melanie Carrico.

Special thanks to my family: Christina May Black, the light of my life; Mom and Dad, the foundation that is never far away; and Michael Leggett, the balance in my life.

Modaris and Diamino for Apparel Design

Basics of Modaris

Modaris is a computer-aided pattern-making program in which the user enters blocks or foundation pattern pieces into the system using a digitizer. The blocks or foundation patterns are then manipulated to produce production patterns, apply pattern grading, and organize the pattern pieces into a style for the marker-making program. This chapter covers some of the basic concepts of Modaris.

In this chapter you will learn about the following:

- Start-Up Procedures
- Opening Modaris
- Modaris Window
- Resizing/Moving the Window
- Using the Mouse
- Files and Directories
- Opening a Model
- Libraries or Access Paths
- Saving a Model File
- Opening a Saved Model File
- Deleting a Saved Model File
- Key Terms and Commands

Start-Up Procedures

Start-up procedures include switching on peripherals such as the digitizing table, plotter, or printer before turning on the computer. Once the computer is turned on, the Windows desktop appears on-screen.

Opening Modaris

The user can open Modaris by clicking the *Start* button at the bottom left task toolbar and scrolling up to *All Programs>Lectra Systems>Modaris* on the pop-up menu. The user can also open Modaris by double-clicking the Modaris shortcut icon on the desktop screen, which is much faster.

The Modaris Window

When Modaris opens, a small pop-up window appears indicating the version of Modaris. Wait and the main working screen opens automatically (Figure 1.1). The large black area, also called the **desktop**, is the work window, which is similar to the pattern-making table. The desktop is where pattern pieces are created, manipulated, or graded.

The screen shows the menu **toolbar** located across the top of the screen. The menu toolbar contains **drop-down menus** with commands specific to the Modaris program. Click the menu options, from file to tool, to open a drop-down menu. Move the cursor down through the drop-down menu to highlight the desired command, and then click the command (Figure 1.2).

The **guided function menu** toolbar located just below the menu toolbar contains semi-automated procedures or tasks commonly used in pattern creation, modification, industrialisation, and grading (Figure 1.3).

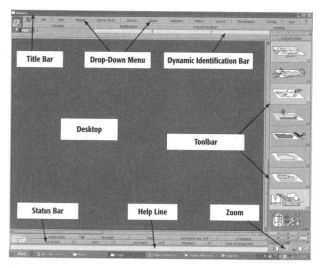

Figure 1.1 The Modaris window showing the title bar, desktop, drop-down menu, dynamic identification bar, toolbar menu, status bar, zoom, and help line.

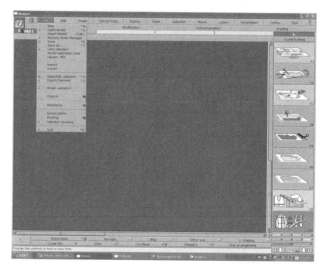

Figure 1.2 Menu bar with drop-down menu.

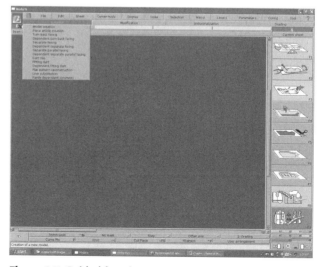

Figure 1.3 Guided function menu.

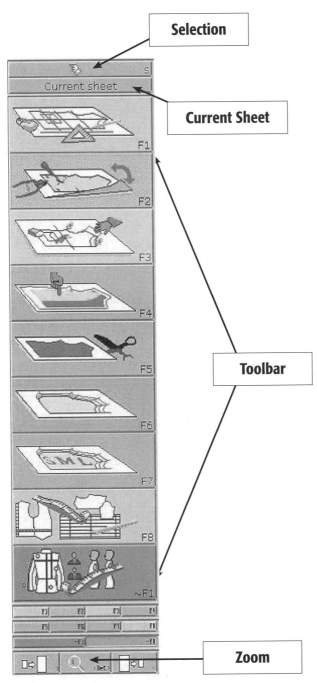

Selection

Current Sheet

Toolbar

Zoom

Figure 1.4 Toolbar menu with selection, current sheet, zoom in, zoom out, and zoom to fit.

Figure 1.5 Dog-ear corner.

The dynamic identification toolbar is located directly under the guided functions menu bar. The toolbar displays the identification data of the sheet, including the name and type of the pattern piece, analytical code, and any comment regarding the pattern piece. To activate the identification toolbar, place the cursor over the pattern piece, and the information is displayed on the toolbar.

The functions toolbar menu is located on the right-hand side of the screen when Modaris first opens, and it contains nine submenus (Figure 1.4). Click one of the toolbar **function buttons** to view command options in a specific submenu. Click a button to activate a command in the toolbar submenus. Specific commands also have "dog-ear corners" (Figure 1.5) that when clicked reveal a dialog or text box that identifies command parameters or that requests additional information. (A dialog box is a submenu that appears after you select a command that has specific information or different settings for a command on-screen. A text box shows the current setting and enables you to edit or type in information such as length, dx, dy, and other angles.) Clicking the dog-ear again closes the dialog box. Click in one of the pink text areas and enter to close a text box. Hint: Text boxes can hide behind the main screen, preventing the user from initiating a new command or action. A gray bullet also indicates parameters associated with a function. Additional buttons above and below the toolbar menu are selection, current sheet, function keys, and zoom buttons.

The **status bar** is located below the desktop (Figure 1.6). It indicates the activated command in the blue area at the left. Shortcuts to selected commands are found along the status bar. The status bar is located directly above the help line. The **help line** in Modaris indicates the required activity for a function tool currently activated. Reading the help line directs the user to the next move.

Resizing/Moving the Window

The title bar menu is located across the top of the window (Figure 1.7). The menu indicates the name of the program, Modaris, and buttons that can change the size of the screen. When Modaris opens, the screen will not be maximized. To enlarge the window to completely fill the computer screen, click the maximize button on the Modaris title bar. The maximize button is the middle of the three buttons on the right side of the title bar. This zooms the window up to full size. To restore a maximized window to its former size, click the restore button that replaces the maximize button. Double-clicking the title bar rather than the buttons will maximize and resize the Modaris screen. The minimize button is the first button on the left in the upper right corner of the window.

The title bar can serve as a handle to move the screen around. To move the entire screen, click and drag the title bar. The screen cannot be moved when it is maximized. The red question mark button at the right end of the drop-down menu bar is the online help button.

Figure 1.6 Status bar menu.

Figure 1.7 Title bar with minimize and maximize buttons.

Using the Mouse

In Modaris, commands are controlled with the left and the right mouse buttons. The left button is used to select, pick, or continue a command. The right button accepts or completes a procedure to end a command. Simultaneously clicking the right and left buttons allows the user to undo steps within a selected command. Hint: Unlike other software programs, Modaris does not close if you click the red button at the right of the title bar.

Files and Directories

Files are used to save pattern pieces in Modaris. Pattern pieces may be saved individually or in a style. Modaris calls styles or files **models**. All files have names and are located in a directory. File names can consist of up to eight characters, with numbers and letters but not symbols. Modaris will automatically assign a file type, with its specific **extension**. For example, *bodicefile* identifies a file that Modaris recognizes as an MDL file name and assigns it an .mdl extension. Before starting pattern making for the first time, you should set up libraries or access paths.

Opening a Model

When you **open** a new model for the first time, a text box appears with the space for the name in the pink area (Figure 1.8). Type the file name and press the Enter key. Hint: The cursor must be in the pink area for a text box to close. If nothing is happening when you are working, check behind large windows to see if a text box is hidden. The first sheet displayed on the desktop is the model that looks like three members in a family (Figure 1.9). In Modaris there are three types of sheets: models, variants, and graphic objects, or the pattern pieces (Figure 1.10).

Saving a Model

After you have opened and worked on a new model (file), you need to save it. The first time you **save a file**, use the *Save As* option. The Save As text box opens and invites you to name a model and choose a folder in which to store the file. Identify the location of a file by the letter of the drive or server, the folder within which it is located, and a unique file name. A typical hard-drive path name could look like this: C:\Modaris\Data\bodice.mdl. The path name is shorthand to indicate that, in the example, a file named bodice.mdl is located in a subfolder called Data, which is in a folder called Modaris, which in turn is on the C drive, or hard drive, of the computer. (The path would be slightly different for saving on a server.) Hint: Saving files frequently is important so work will not be lost. Use *Save As* to check the file path.

Figure 1.8 Opening a model text box.

Figure 1.9 Model sheet displayed on the desktop.

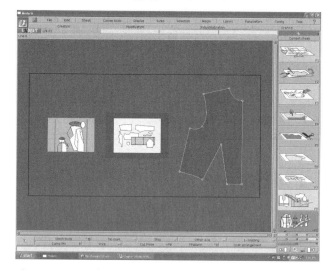

Figure 1.10 Model, variant, and pattern piece sheets displayed on the desktop.

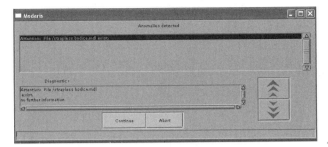

Figure 1.11 Saving a model or file.

Saving a File for the First Time

1. Select *File>Save As* from the drop-down menu.

2. Find and select the folder where the model is to be saved. The default path for an individual computer is usually C:\ Modaris\Data. The Save As text box appears.

3. Modaris requires a name for the file. Place your cursor in the File Name text box to type your file name.

4. Click the Save button.

Saving a Previously Saved File

1. If the file was saved previously, select *File>Save* from the drop-down menu. You will be asked whether to overwrite the file.

2. If you want to save your most recent work, click *Continue* with the left mouse button. *Abort* does not make changes to the file and reverts back to your most recent work (Figure 1.11).

Opening a Saved Model File

As mentioned, in Modaris, files are referred to as models. Therefore, to open a file, you must select the correct model.

Opening a Model File

1. Choose *File>Open* from the drop-down menu.

2. Open the correct folder, and find the document you want to open. Hint: Remember, the default path for an individual computer is usually C:\Modaris\ Data. The *Open* dialog box appears when you click the Modaris icon of the required file. Select open or double-click on the file name to open the file.

Deleting a Saved Model File

Good file management requires the removal of unneeded files and folders to free up hard drive or server space.

Deleting a Model File

1. Go to *My Computer* and open the folder that holds the Modaris files or folders you want to **delete**. Files can be located on the server or the hard drive.

2. Choose the files you want to delete by highlighting the file or folder.

3. Choose *File>Delete* from the drop-down menu, or press the Delete key on your keyboard. Another method is to right-click the file to activate the pop-up menu and click Delete. Files can also be deleted by dragging them to the recycle bin.

4. In the dialog box that appears, click the Yes button to confirm that you want to delete the file and send it to the recycle bin.

Exercises

1. Open the folder from the CD-ROM and open the file named Chapter 1 Practice.

2. Use the mouse to move the pieces around on-screen.

3. Identify the drop-down menus, the guided function menus, and the toolbar menus.

4. Identify the desktop, help line, and a dog-ear of a toolbar command.

5. Save the Chapter 1 Practice file under another file name.

Key Terms and Commands

Desktop

Drop-down menu

File

File delete

File extension

File save

Function buttons

Guided function menu

Help line

Model

Open model

Save model

Status bar

Toolbar

Getting Started

2

This chapter outlines the key terms, definitions, menus, and toolbar functions. The chapter also focuses on the general commands used in pattern making. The commands in this chapter serve as the foundation for the Modaris program and pattern-making exercises. Similar to other computer programs, Modaris allows the user to apply the same commands or solutions in a variety of ways. For example, patterns can be digitized into the computer, created on-screen, opened as previously saved files, or imported from another file. Further explanation of commands can also be found in chapters with related activities and in Appendix A.

In this chapter you will learn about the following:

- General Terms and Definitions
- Common Keyboard Commands
- Drop-Down Menus
- Guided Function Menus
- Toolbar Menu
- Zoom
- Key Terms and Commands

General Terms and Definitions

Construction lines are the white lines of a pattern.

A **model** is a file created in Modaris that holds all the pattern pieces, including flat pattern pieces and variants that belong to one style.

A **variant** belongs to a model and holds the list of shapes that creates one style variation. One model can have one or several variants. It specifies each shape, fabric type, and number of pieces to be cut, as well as other cutting information. A variant in the Modaris system is the apparel industry's version of a "cutter's must" (see Chapter 8).

A **flat pattern** is a series of points and lines that create a shape. The flat pattern is only the white lines and is not solid blue in color.

A **basic image (BI)** is a pattern piece.

A **garment** is a list of basic images belonging to a garment and is generated from a variant.

A **piece article** is referenced to a pattern piece that belongs to a model.

A **shape** is one pattern piece.

A **sheet** holds the shape and all of its information.

The **title block** is the yellow field surrounding the sheet that holds the shapes and information regarding the pattern (see Chapter 3).

Common Keyboard Commands

The following keyboard commands and shortcuts assist in viewing pattern pieces on the desktop. Open the Chapter 2 Practice file provided on the CD-ROM, and try each of the following commands. For each command, select the key on the keyboard.

Desk Arrange organizes pattern pieces on the desktop. Select *End* on the keyboard.

End arranges pattern pieces on the desktop. While working, press the End key on your keyboard, and then move the required pieces

.closer together. Note: The pieces do not stay permanently in the new arrangement.

Home centers on a selected pattern piece on the desktop.

J arranges all the pattern pieces on the desktop.

Page Down allows you to view the next sheet in order on the desktop. You can view one sheet at a time.

Page Up allows you to view the previous sheet in order on the desktop. You can view one sheet at a time.

. (period) allows you to view all pattern pieces on the desktop. The pieces are not reshuffled when the period is used.

s (lowercase) deselects the activated function that you are currently using. The *Selection* command can also be found under the **Display drop-down menu** at the top of the

screen, as well as at the top of the **toolbar function menu**.

z deletes a sheet. The *Delete* command can also be found under the **Sheet drop-down menu** at the top of the screen.

i selects a sheet. You can also select a sheet by right-clicking it.

a resizes a sheet. Select a sheet and then select the *a* key on the keyboard. Sheets need to be made smaller after certain commands such as *Marry*.

P displays curve points. Curve points can also be found under the *Display* drop-down menu at the top of the screen.

Spacebar can change direction of commands or functions, including changing direction when you place a point on a line onto an adjacent line of a pattern piece.

Drop-Down Menus

The drop-down menu options are found along the top of the Modaris screen (Figure 2.1). You open drop-down menus by clicking on the keywords, starting with *File* at the left-hand side to *Tool* on the right-hand side. Drop-down menus may also have submenus that can be accessed by hovering the cursor over arrows found to the right of selected drop-down options (Figure 2.2). Commands under drop-down menus can be found in the chapters with specific activities, and full descriptions of commands are in Appendix A. The commands described in this chapter allow the user to start working in Modaris.

Similar to other software programs, the **File menu** contains file-related options including *New, Open Model, Save, Save As,* and *Quit* functions. As mentioned in the previous chapter, in Modaris, a file is referred to as a model. Therefore, *New* creates a model never before saved, and *Open Model* opens a previously saved model. *Insert Model* allows the insertion of a whole model or pattern pieces, including the variant, into another model. *Save As* allows work to be saved with a different name and in a different location. Once work has been saved, the *Save* command can be used to resave work. Hint: Check the path using *Save As* before leaving the program. Searching for a lost file on a server is like searching for the proverbial needle in a haystack. Hint: Save your work often! With the *Import BI (basic image) Model* command, pattern pieces or models can be combined with other pattern pieces or models. *Quit*, located at the bottom of the *File* menu, must be used to exit the Modaris program. Unlike other Windows programs, the red X in the upper right corner of the program's window cannot be used to exit.

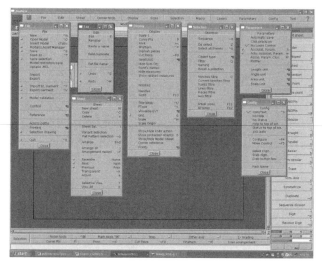

Figure 2.1 Drop-down menus.

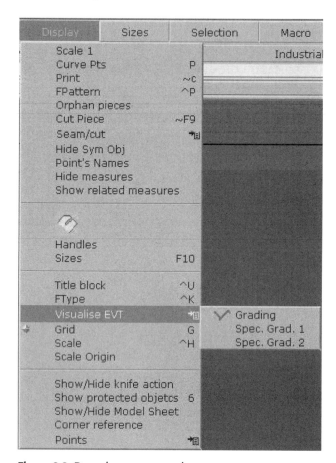

Figure 2.2 Drop-down menu and pop-up menu.

The **Edit menu** enables the user to change previous work. Commands in the *Edit* menu include *Edit, Rename, Undo,* and *Redo. Edit* and *Rename* can be input directly on the pattern piece. Chapter 6 covers the steps for naming and renaming pattern pieces. Labeling is important for pattern identification. Pattern pieces and variant names are limited to a maximum of eight characters. *Undo* cancels the last operation. You can cancel *Undo* by selecting *Redo*. The *Edit>Undo* and *Edit>Redo* commands work with commands located in the toolbar menu.

The *Sheet* menu changes how patterns are viewed on the desktop. Sheets on the desktop can be newly created, copied, deleted, selected, arranged, adjusted, or resized. *Recenter* positions only the selected pattern piece on-screen, as does Home on the keyboard. A*djust* reconfigures the size of an individual sheet to the smallest size possible. Changing to view a different sheet or pattern can be as simple as selecting *previous* or *next*. The same viewing change can be accomplished by pressing Page Up or Page Down on the keyboard. A sheet can be selected under the *Sheet* menu, the selection button above the toolbar menu, or by right-clicking the mouse to select a sheet. *Sheet Selection* is a neutral option between commands but is not necessary. Note: It is good to go to *Sheet Selection* when you get lost in a command. Also, note that the icon changes to a skull and crossbones when *Sheet Delete* is selected.

The *Corner Tools* menu enables the user to select the type of corner to complete pattern seam allowances. Changing the corners of the seam allowances is covered in Chapter 6, "Completing a Pattern."

The *Display* menu enables the user to show or hide items on the desktop such as curve points, print for the original plot lines of a pattern piece, notches, the title block, seams, cut pieces, or a grid. You can display the desktop at a scale of one or display a grid for improved accuracy in pattern making. When you toggle the *Grid* command, the grid is displayed in the background and then on the pattern piece after you have selected the first point. The *Display* menu shows the user but does not allow the user to change what is seen. For example, with the *Curve Points* command under the *Display* menu, you can view curve points but not change them (Figure 2.3). As mentioned, the title block is the yellow field surrounding a sheet that you can toggle on or off when working. The *Title Block* menu displays information about a pattern on the sheet it is attached to (see Chapter 3).

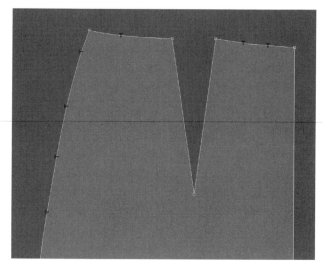

Figure 2.3 Curve points.

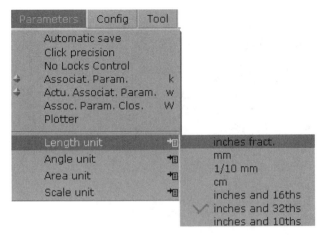

Figure 2.4 *Parameters* drop-down menu.

The **Parameters menu** enables the user to choose characteristics including automatic save and unit options. The *Length Unit* option creates and measures the images on the desktop in centimeters or inches. The path to change the unit of measurement is *Parameters>Length Unit>inches and 32ths* (yes, not 32nds) (Figure 2.4). Therefore, seam allowances are calculated in 32nds of an inch. This means that a seam allowance of $1/2''$ is $16/32''$; therefore, for $1/2$, you would enter "16" as the numerator. Table 2.1 indicates common measurements and the equivalent in 32nds of an inch.

Table 2.1 Conversion Chart

Common Measurements	16th Inch	32nds Inch
	$1/16$	$2/32$
$1/8$	$2/16$	$4/32$
	$3/16$	$6/32$
$1/4$	$4/16$	$8/32$
	$5/16$	$10/32$
$3/8$	$6/16$	$12/32$
	$7/16$	$14/32$
$1/2$	$8/16$	$16/32$
	$9/16$	$18/32$
$5/8$	$10/16$	$20/32$
	$11/16$	$22/32$
$3/4$	$12/16$	$24/32$
	$13/16$	$26/32$
$7/8$	$14/16$	$28/32$
	$15/16$	$30/32$
$8/8$	$16/16$	$32/32$

Depending on the country of the user, manufacturer, or marketplace, it may be easier, more time-efficient, and more consistent to permanently change the length instead of the parameter each time Modaris is opened.

The **Config(ure) menu** enables the user to arrange the items viewed, including the toolbar menu and submenu. Select either pictures or words for the toolbar menu display option by toggling the *Icon>Text* command back and forth. Most users prefer either the images or the text. When you first open the Modaris *Config* menu, the command is displayed with icons. To change icons to text, select *Config* and click on *Icon/Text* (Figure 2.5). Text is activated when the red check is visible on the menu. The icons are activated when there is no red check.

Modaris settings have automatic defaults that activate when the program opens. Take time to review the drop-down menus. After learning the defaults, you can modify settings by creating a program folder on the hard drive or server to configure the settings locally. This will permanently change the default settings when you open the Modaris program.

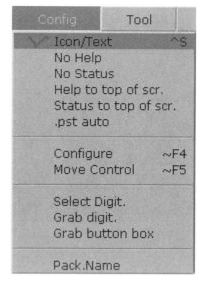

Figure 2.5 *Config* drop-down menu.

Guided Function Menus

The **guided function menu** bar, or macro, contains semiautomated tasks or procedures commonly used in pattern creation, modification, industrialisation, and grading (Figure 2.6). The guided functions are excellent learning tools that save time for recurring tasks, and they can also be modified to meet a company's needs.

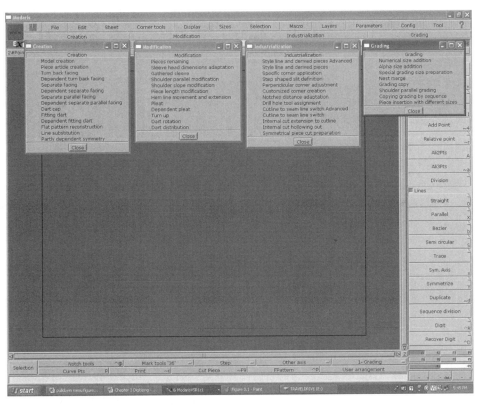

Figure 2.6 Guided function menus.

Click the desired heading, and select the function or pattern change in the menu. A dialog box opens displaying instructions or easy-to-follow steps. The user enters parameters or values for some functions or procedures. The guided function menus can assist the user when learning the Modaris program by guiding the user through selected commands.

Toolbar Menu

Function commands are used to create, modify, or grade pattern pieces (Figures 2.7a and b). Function commands can also be activated with the function buttons, and many can be activated by keyboard shortcuts (see Table 2.2).

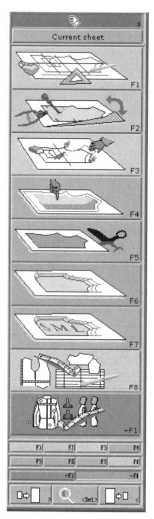

Figure 2.7a Icon toolbar menu.

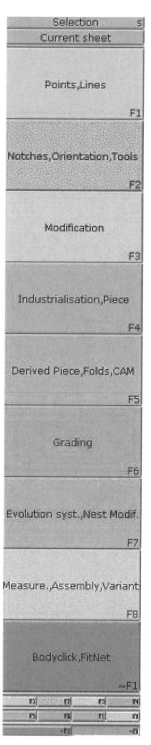

Figure 2.7b Text toolbar menu.

Table 2.2 Function Key Commands

Function Key	Menus and Commands
F1	Points and Lines
F2	Notches, Orientation, and Tools
F3	Deletion, Line modification, Point modification, and Pins
F4	Industrialisation and Piece
F5	Derived pieces, Folds
F6	Grading control, Grading modification, and Grading rules
F7	Evolution system and Nest modification
F8	Measurement, Assembly, and Variant
F9	Graded nest display
F10	Displays only the base size, no brading
F11	Displays the break sizes of grading
F12	Displays all sizes of grading

Table 2.3 Point Characteristics

Point Type	Characteristics
X	Blue is a graded point that could be a characteristic, curve, or linked point, an absolute point.
X	Red curve point.
X	White is a nongraded point that could be a characteristic, curve, or linked point.
▢	A beginning/endpoint of a line. Each pattern piece requires at least two points for a shape. Beginning and endpoints are usually placed on corners or end of line segments.
◯	Slider point that slides along a contour line without modifying it.
▷	Developed point that is dependent on a reference point.
◯	Intersection point that is placed at two crossing lines. Pinned point (also unattached points).
◇	Red pinned point.

You can find functions relating to points and lines under the menu activated by pressing F1. With the F1 choices, different types of points can be input and points can be aligned. Table 2.3 outlines the types of points in Modaris and their characteristics. The type of point used depends on the placement of the point. Slider, developed, and intersection points can only be placed on a line; relative points can be used on a line or inside the lines of a pattern piece. Figure 2.8a shows the various types of points that can be used in Modaris. You can select point types at the dog-ear corner of selected points. A dialog box allows the user to choose the point type by checking it (Figure 2.8b). A red check indicates the selection. You can draw lines by using the F1 functions—straight, curved, or a combination of straight and curved.

The third function under F1 is *Digitizing*, which allows you to input pattern pieces into the computer. Chapter 3 outlines the basics of digitizing.

Functions relating to notches, orientation of pattern pieces, and tool or shape commands are found under F2. Notches can be added, oriented in a specific direction, and modified. When making patterns, you can select four types of notches. Orientation commands allow you to reposition pattern pieces by rotation or symmetry. Tool commands can be used to create basic shapes such as rectangles and circles in order to develop pattern pieces such as pockets, cuffs, collars, and circular skirts on-screen. See Chapter 6, "Completing a Pattern," for examples.

Functions relating to pattern modifications are located under F3. You can use these commands to change or correct pattern pieces on the desktop by changing points or lines.

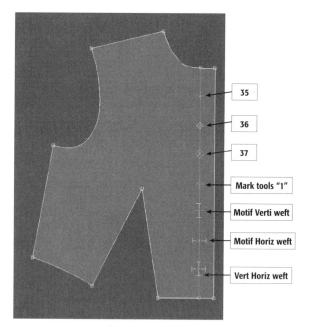

Figure 2.8a Point selection.

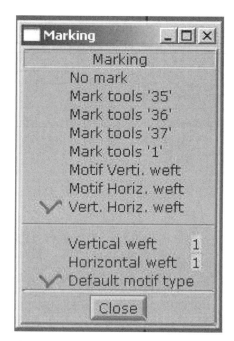

Figure 2.8b Points dialog box.

Functions relating to *Industrialisation* and *Pieces* are found under F4. *Industrialisation* is the addition or deletion of seam allowances, creation of shaped seams and corners, and data modification. *Pieces* commands also allow the definition of construction lines as seam lines or cut lines.

Functions relating to *Derived Pieces* and *Folds* are located under F5. *Derived pieces* are by definition patterns of pieces created from existing pattern pieces. *Fold* commands are used to create darts, folds, or pleats. *Pleat* commands can also be used for adding fullness to a pattern piece.

Pattern Grading commands are located under F6. These commands are used to resize shapes, create grade rules, and grade pattern pieces. Chapter 7 outlines the principles of pattern grading.

Functions relating to *Evolution System* and *Nest Modifications* are located in the F7 submenu. *Evolution System* commands are used in the creation and modification of size ranges, including numeric and alphanumeric size tables. *Nest Modifications* commands are used in the manipulation of size ranges of graded shapes.

Functions relating to *Measurements, Assembly,* and *Variants* are found under F8. *Measurements* are tools for measuring shapes and spreadsheets for recording measurements of a pattern. *Assembly* commands compare one pattern piece with another for final checking. *Assembly* can be used to true pattern pieces. *Variants* commands affect the creation of all garments, including shapes, amounts, and fabrics. Variants are used in marker making (see Chapter 8). To return to the main function menu, press F8.

Zoom

As indicated in Figure 1.4 of Chapter 1, the three gray buttons at the bottom of the toolbar menu are **zoom** buttons. The middle button is for creating a window to zoom around a selected object or zoom to fit. Click at the outer edge of an object and drag the mouse until the box surrounds the object to be enlarged. The right button of the three is used to zoom out, and the left button is used to zoom in. Hint: Zoom is extremely important for accuracy and for viewing pattern changes more clearly.

Exercises

1. Review the commands found under the drop-down menus.

2. Review the toolbar commands.

3. Change the toolbar functions from Icons to Text.

4. Open the folder from the CD-ROM, and open the file named Chapter 2 Practice. Practice zooming in, zooming out, and zooming using the box to view a selected area of the pattern pieces.

5. Create a new sheet on-screen.

Key Terms and Commands

a	P
Basic image (BI)	Page Down
Config(ure) menu	Page Up
Construction lines	Parameters menu
Desk arrange	. (period)
Display drop-down menu	Piece article
End	s (lowercase)
Edit menu	Shape
Flat pattern	Sheet
File menu	Sheet drop-down menu
Garment	Spacebar
Guided function menu	Title block
Home	Toolbar function menu
i	Variant
J	z
Model	Zoom

Digitizing in Modaris

3

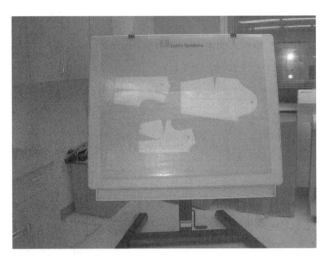

Figure 3.1 Digitizing table.

Digitizing is the inputting of hard copy pattern pieces, slopers, or blocks into the computer. Digitizing is the pattern maker's method of scanning. Accuracy and consistency are the keys to good digitizing. The more accurate the digitizing, the fewer corrections that will be required when you are creating an original pattern or design. In pattern making, digitizers are the size of large tables (Figure 3.1).

In this chapter you will learn about the following:

- Commands in Digitizing
- Toolbar Commands for Pattern Corrections
- Commands for Sizing a Pattern
- Drop-Down Menu Commands
- The Mouse
- Pattern Preparation
- Digitizing Fundamentals
- Digitizing a Symmetrical Pattern Piece
- Digitizing an Oversize Pattern Piece
- Pattern Corrections after Digitizing
- Title Block
- Size Tables
- Key Terms and Commands

Commands in Digitizing

F1>Lines>Digit is used to manually digitize a shape into the computer. Before digitizing, click the dog-ear corner to bring up the dialog box. Select *No Flat Pat.* to eliminate the generation of the flat pattern during digitizing. The flat pattern appears on the desktop as a white outline of a pattern piece.

F1>Lines>Recover Digit automatically activates when you define the horizontal axis line.

Toolbar Commands for Pattern Corrections

The following are toolbar commands commonly used to correct patterns after digitizing. Going through basic pattern corrections after digitizing will reduce problems later in the pattern-making process.

F1>Points>Add Point adds a characteristic point or a **curve point** at a relative distance from a reference or point. Click a point, then move the cursor to a new position and click.

F1>Points>Relative point places a new point in or on the style relative to the first click or anchor point. Click a point on a line or inside the pattern piece, then move the cursor to the new position and click.

F1>Points>Ali2Pts orients a pattern piece according to a horizontal or vertical axis relative to a reference point. Click the hem/center front intersection point and then the hem/side seam intersection point.

F1>Points>Ali3Pts aligns a point along a line defined by two reference points. To align the shoulder seam, click the shoulder/armhole intersection point, then the shoulder/neckline intersection point, and lastly the point in the middle of the shoulder seam.

F2>Notches>Notch places notches along a line. Click a point to place a notch.

F2>Notches>Orientation reorients a notch by pivoting the notch end. Zoom in close to select the notch.

F2>Notches>Perpendicular orients a notch at 90 degrees to the line where it is attached. Click the notch, and it automatically orients to the line.

F2>Orientation>X sym flips a piece from top to bottom. Click the Xsym button and select the sheet to flip.

F2>Orientation>Y sym flips a piece from right to left. Click the Ysym button and select the sheet to flip.

F2>Orientation >30>–30>45>–45>90>–90>180 enables rotation at the specific degrees identified. Click the orientation button, and select the sheet to flip.

F2>Orientation>Rot 2pt rotates the entire pattern piece horizontally between two points such as endpoints on the center front seam. Click the pattern piece to activate the change. Hint: To undo orientation commands, use the function in the opposite direction, not the undo button.

F3>Deletion removes points and internal lines from a pattern piece. Click the point or line to remove.

F3>Line Modification>Simplify reduces the number of points between two points along a curved line—for example, to smooth or change the shape of a sleeve cap. Click two points along a curved line; a text box opens. The tolerance appears in the pink area of the text box and is the amount of variation in the line between two points. You can modify this by typing a new amount into the text box.

F3>Point Modification>Reshape is used to change the shape of an existing pattern piece. Click a point and move the cursor to the desired position, then click to set the point in the new position. To move a point a precise amount, use the text box by typing in the amount the point is to change.

F5>Derived pieces>Sym2Pts generates the symmetry of either a whole or part of a pattern piece. A new piece is generated.

Commands for Sizing a Pattern

F7>Evolution System>Imp.EVT is used to import a size range for a new style. Click the **model sheet** (sheet with the yellow) to bring up the file directory.

F7>Evolution System>Rep.EVT is used to add sizing to all sheets in a file. Choose *Selection>Select all sheets*, and click all the sheets that require sizing in the file, then select *F7>Evolution System>Rep.EVT* and choose the sizing required.

F8>Measurement>Length measures the length between two points on a line, either straight or curved. Click the first point and then on the second point.

Drop-Down Menu Commands

Drop-down menu commands commonly used in digitizing to create sheets or correct patterns after digitizing include the following:

Sheet>New sheet adds a new sheet to the desktop. Click the desktop to create the new sheet.

Sheet>Delete removes a sheet from the desktop. To remove a sheet from the desktop, click the sheet.

Edit>Redo restores the last function.

Sheet>Recenter organizes the pattern pieces on the desktop.

Edit>Undo reverses the last function, move, or task under the *Sheet* drop-down menu.

The Mouse

The **mouse** in Figure 3.2 is designed for digitizing. The mouse has an X or crosshair lines for accurate alignment with the pattern edge or internal markings, as well as buttons designed for steps required in digitizing a pattern. When inputting the pattern piece or sloper onto the desktop, the user uses the mouse to digitize points. The points indicate the external and internal points of a pattern piece. Table 3.1 shows the command functions of the digitizing mouse.

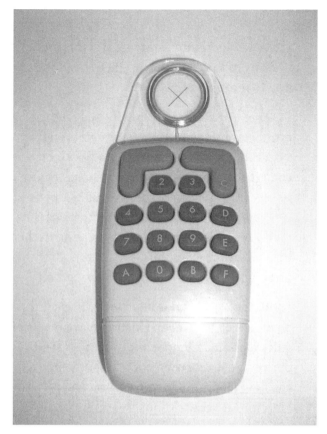

Figure 3.2 Digitizing mouse.

Table 3.1 Digitizing Mouse Commands

Key	Characteristic	Key	Characteristic
1	Characteristic point	B	Toggle pivot Bezier/Semicircular
2	Begin/endpoint of a line segment	C	Curve point
3	Internal mark/drill hole	D	Undo, cancels the last operation
4	Pattern hook hole	E	Input rule name
5	Input notch/mark type	F	End digitizing; end internal line
6	Notch	I	Input DL, rotation (on the keyboard)
7	Beginning internal line/End internal cut	O	Multiple sheet digitizing
8	Reference axis	X	Input DX, DY, and rotation (on the keyboard)
9	Orients an internal notch		
A	Beginning and end of the horizontal x-axis (left to right and must be at least 1" in length)	↓	Input values in X, Y, DL, DY (on the keyboard)

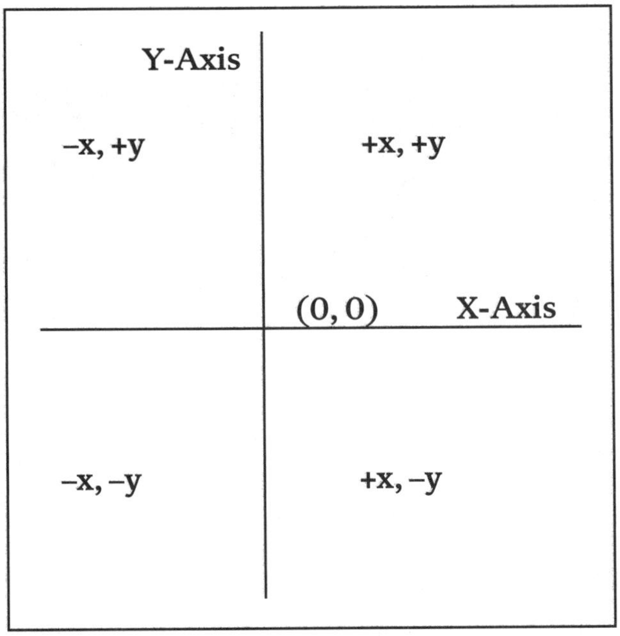

Figure 3.3 Cartesian graph.

Some commands on the digitizing buttons on the mouse are required for pattern grading. Pattern grading is covered in Chapter 7, as is digitizing a graded nest. The computer is based on the **Cartesian graph**, which contains a horizontal x-axis and a vertical y-axis, as indicated in Figure 3.3. As a pattern piece is digitized, Dx and Dy coordinates are assigned to identify point placement on a pattern. DL represents the distance between sizes. The Cartesian coordinate system is explained further in Chapter 7. The orientation of a pattern piece must be consistent in placement for digitizing and pattern grading.

Pattern Preparation

Before digitizing, pattern pieces or slopers need to be prepared, particularly curved areas. Placement or positioning of curve points and notches along curved seams is important, since the correct placement will create a smooth seam line that requires less correction afterward.

When you are placing the points along a curved seam, the goal is to maintain a smooth, accurate seam line. Using too many curved points or placing curved points too close together will distort a line. The smoother the line when digitizing, the fewer the pattern corrections that will be required after digitizing. The pattern piece or sloper is placed under the plastic cover on the digitizer after curve points have been calculated.

Calculating Curved Point Placement

1. Line 1 is a straight line between the two endpoints of a curved line (Figure 3.4).

2. Line 2 is located at the deepest part of the curve between the two endpoints of Line 1. Line 2 should be placed at the deepest distance from the curved line. Line 2 is located at a right angle to Line 1. For example, Line 2 in Figure 3.4 is at the deepest placement of the curve, or at midpoint between the armhole/shoulder seam and the armhole/underarm seam intersection points. Point A is created along the curved line at the intersection of Line 2.

3. Lines 3 and 4 are created by connecting Point A with the two original endpoints of the curved line.

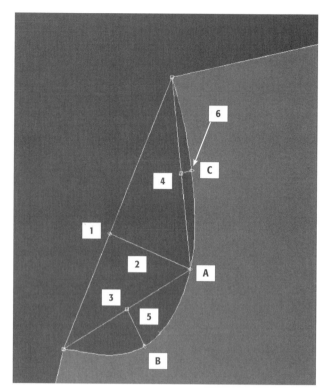

Figure 3.4 Line placement for curve points.

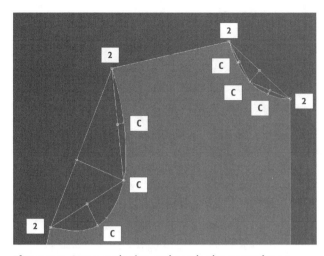

Figure 3.5 Curve, endpoint, and notch placement for an armhole and neckline.

4. Lines 5 and 6 are placed at the deepest points along lines 3 and 4. Lines 5 and 6 are at right angles to lines 3 and 4. Points B and C are found at the intersection of lines 3 and 4 and the curved line. Figure 3.5 indicates the point types along a curve line. Figure 3.6 is an example of the points used to digitize a torso block.

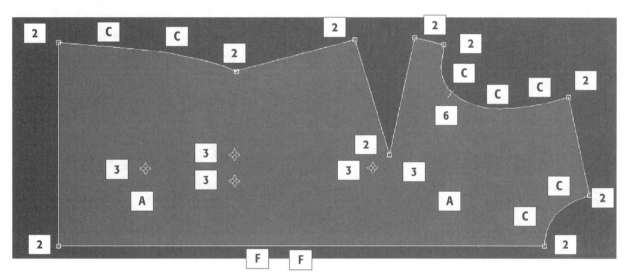

Figure 3.6 Points for digitizing a torso.

Digitizing Fundamentals

Digitizing must be done at a computer that is directly connected to a digitizer. To digitize a pattern piece, you must enter at least two type 2 points. *Type 2 points* indicate the beginning and end of line segments and are represented by a white square on the pattern pieces.

At the Computer

1. Open *File>New* to open a new model. When the model is opened, the model sheet (looks like a family) appears on-screen.

2. Select *Sheet>New sheet*.

3. Select *F1>Lines>Digit*. Click the dog-ear corner to bring up the dialog box. Select *No Flat Pat.* to eliminate the generation of the flat pattern during digitizing (Figure 3.7). A flat pattern appears on the desktop as a white outline of a pattern piece.

4. Click the new sheet. The sheet is ready when the phrase "2 Points for horizontal axis" appears at the upper left corner of the desktop (Figure 3.8). Hint: To exit *Digit*, right-click the desktop.

5. Move to the digitizer.

At the Digitizer

1. Place a pattern piece horizontally on the digitizer. The plastic cover is designed to hold a pattern piece or pieces in place when digitizing. Note: Do not pin or use other methods to hold pattern pieces in place.

2. Using the digitizing mouse, at the left end of the grain line, press the *A* key one time, then press *A* at the right end of grain line. This creates a green horizontal grain line on the computer screen (Figure 3.9). The longer the grain line, the more accurate the placement of the pattern piece on the y-axis. Digitize the grain line horizontally from left to right. Digitizing the grain line

Figure 3.7 *Digit. Param.* (digitizing parameters) dialog box.

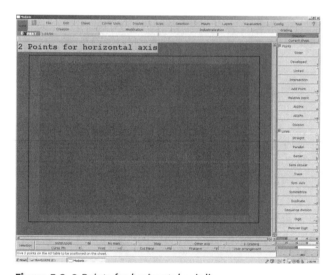

Figure 3.8 *2 Points for horizontal axis* line.

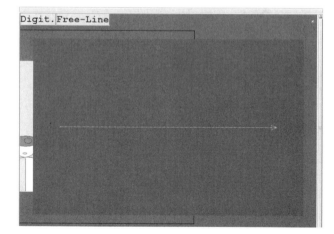

Figure 3.9 Digit. Free-Line or grain line.

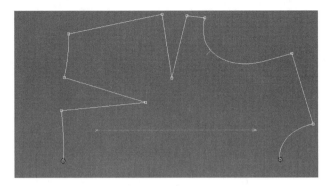

Figure 3.10 Bodice front draft.

from right to left inputs the mirror image of the pattern piece on the screen (or the reverse of the placement of the pattern piece on the digitizer).

3. You need to digitize systematically, adding points in a clockwise direction. Pattern pieces can be digitized starting at any corner point and ending at the same point. For example, start at the lower left corner of a pattern piece, and press *2* on the digitizing mouse to begin a line segment. Moving in a clockwise direction, continue to input the numbers required for a specific pattern piece.

4. Before closing a pattern piece, add in all additional internal lines. Before you close the pattern piece, a pattern draft appears on-screen (Figure 3.10).

5. To finish or close a pattern piece, type *FF* with the digitizing mouse, holding the mouse on the digitizing table. *Hint:* The mouse can be placed anywhere on the digitizing table.

6. To continue digitizing additional pattern pieces, select *Sheet>New sheet.* A new sheet must be placed on-screen before you digitize additional pattern pieces. If the sheet appears small, press Home on the computer keyboard to enlarge the sheet. Digitizing can also be done with a small sheet on-screen. Once all the pattern pieces have been digitized, select **Sheet>Arrange all** to arrange the pieces on-screen.

7. Save your file.

Missing internal points or drill holes can be added after a pattern piece has been digitized. Place the pattern piece back on the digitizing table. Select the pattern piece on-screen to indicate it as the current sheet. Select *Digit*. Validate the two reference points. The two reference points are the A A that originally created the grain line. Digitize the internal points and press *FF* on the digitizing mouse to finish, keeping the mouse on the digitizing table, or enter only one *F* if you have other pattern pieces to digitize.

Digitizing a Symmetrical Pattern Piece

For accuracy, digitize half of a symmetrical pattern piece, such as a back, taking care to begin and end digitizing at the exact center back (center front) of the pattern piece. If the beginning and end of the pattern piece are not at the exact center back (center front), the piece will be too big or too small.

Creating a Full Symmetrical Pattern Piece

1. If a full pattern piece is required for a design, select *F5>Derived pieces>Sym2pts*.

2. Click the two points that create the axis. This will create a full front or back pattern piece.

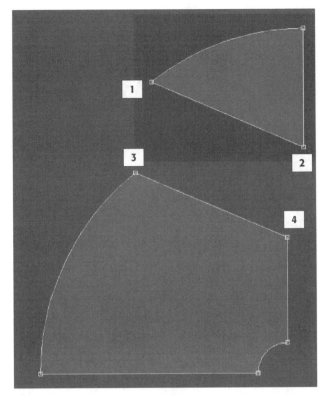

Figure 3.11 Joining pattern pieces.

Digitizing an Oversize Pattern Piece

Digitizing an oversize pattern piece enables the user to digitize pattern pieces of any size. Separating a pattern piece for digitizing should only be done when a whole piece will not fit on the digitizer. The oversize piece is divided into any number of smaller parts, and then each part is digitized in.

Digitizing an Oversize Piece

1. Mark any necessary cut lines for the partial pattern pieces to fit on the table. Divide the pattern piece into as few parts as possible.

2. Digitize the first partial pattern piece, ending with *FO* on the digitizing mouse. Ending with *FO* rather than *FF* will allow the second partial piece to be digitized.

3. Digitize the second partial pattern piece. Continue until all the partial pattern pieces have been digitized.

At the Computer

After all the parts of the pattern piece are digitized into the computer, return to the computer and complete the following steps:

1. To attach the partial pattern pieces together, select **F5>Derived Pieces>Join**. Figure 3.11 indicates the order in which to click the endpoints to join two pattern pieces together. A new pattern piece is derived. Joining pattern pieces is explained further in Chapter 4.

2. Select *Sheet>Delete* to remove the partial pattern pieces. Hint: Hold the Shift key down to delete all pattern layers at one time.

Pattern Corrections after Digitizing

After you digitize basic patterns, corrections such as trueing and creating right angles may be required. The following are basic pattern corrections that should be done before starting pattern manipulations. Hint: Check patterns for accuracy before starting any pattern manipulations to save time later on.

When you select a pattern piece, either with the right mouse button or with the selection button at the top of the function toolbar, the pattern piece turns green (Figure 3.12). When you select a different pattern piece, the pattern piece turns blue.

Pattern Corrections

1. To obtain a correct pattern orientation, select *F3>Points>Rotate 2pts*, and click the two endpoints on center front from left to right. This orients the pattern piece on the straight of grain in the horizontal direction.

2. The center front and hemline should be at right angles; select *F1>Points>Ali2Pts* to obtain a right angle. Click the two endpoints of the hem, first the hem/center front intersection point and then the hem/side seam intersection point.

3. To create a straight shoulder seam, select *F1>Points>Ali3Pts*. Click the shoulder/armhole intersection point, then the shoulder/neckline intersection point, and lastly the point in the middle of the shoulder seam. This should be done when the shoulder seam has a notch.

Figure 3.12 Selected pattern piece turns green. (See Chapter Art folder in Chapter 3 on CD-ROM.)

Figure 3.13 Curve points.

Figure 3.14 *Line modification>Simplify* activates this text box.

4. Curve seams may need to be trued to create a smooth seam line. Zoom to display the curved seam. Select *Display> Curve Pts* to indicate the position of the curve points situated along the seam line (Figure 3.13). Select *F3>Modification> Reshape,* and correct the seam line by clicking on the red curve points and then moving the mouse to the desired position. Left-click to end the command and to make the move permanent. You can add more points to a seam line in order to smooth a curve by selecting *F1>Points>Add Point.* Hint: If too many points have been added during digitizing, select *F3>Deletion* to remove extra points. Click a point to delete.

5. To smooth a curved line, select *F3>Line modification>Simplify* and click the line. A text box appears. Type in the amount of tolerance desired on the line variation (Figure 3.14).

Title Block

As mentioned in the previous chapter, the title block is the yellow field surrounding a sheet that holds the sizing, shapes, and information regarding a pattern piece (Figure 3.15). Title blocks are attached to each sheet found in a model. There are two types of title blocks: At the left of the sheet is the evolution or size system title block, and at the bottom is the sheet identification title block. The model, variant, and pattern sheets contain title block information related to the specific sheets.

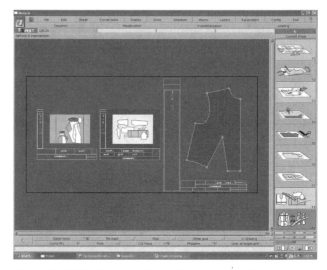

Figure 3.15 Title blocks with model, variant, and pattern piece.

Creating or Modifying a Title Block

1. Open *File>New* to open a new model. The model sheet (family) is displayed on the screen.

2. Select *Display>Title Block* to display the title block.

3. Select *F7> Evolution System>Imp.EVT*. If size tables have been created, click the model sheet to bring up the file directory. Select a size file from the size table folder provided on the CD-ROM. Sizing pattern pieces can be done before or after digitizing pattern pieces.

4. If the sizing has not been added to all the sheets in a file, select *Selection>Select all sheets*; then select *F7>Evolution system> Rep.EVT* and choose the sizes required by selecting a size table.

5. An alphanumeric EVT can be converted into a numeric EVT. Select *F7>Evolution System>numeric.EVT*, and then click the file name of the EVT to be converted.

6. A numeric EVT can be converted into an alphanumeric EVT. Select *F7>Evolution System>alpha.EVT*, and then click the file name of the EVT to be converted.

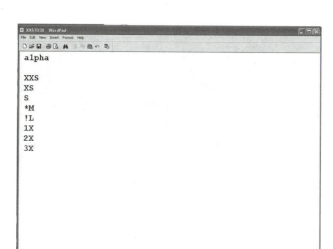

Figure 3.16a Alpha text file.

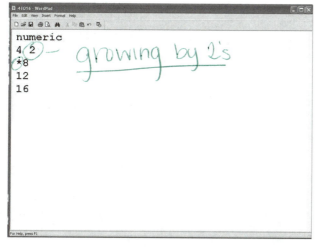

Figure 3.16b Numeric text file.

7. The title block can be turned on or off when you are digitizing or working on a pattern. Select *Display>Title Block* to toggle it on and off.

Size Tables

Two types of sizing systems can be created in Lectra: alpha (Figure 3.16a) and numeric (Figure 3.16b). **Alpha sizing** is represented by lettering such as S, M, and L. **Numeric sizing** is represented by numbers such as 2, 4, 6, and 8.

Sizing files are used for pattern grading to indicate the range and sizes of pattern pieces and models (Figures 3.17a and b). Once sizes of a garment or pattern piece are selected, they are displayed on the desktop in the title block. Table 3.2 indicates the symbols used in size files. The symbols are used with the actual numbers that represent the size range of the garment.

Creating a Text File

1. Select *Start>Programs>Accessories> Notepad*. Size files are created using text. Use lowercase letters in Notepad or WordPad.

2. Select *File>New* to open a text document.

3. Type in the text for alpha sizing or numeric garment sizing.

4. Name the file and save it in a text folder. Alphanumeric tables are identified by a name followed by an .eva (EVA) extension. The numeric tables are identified by a name followed by an .evn (EVN) extension.

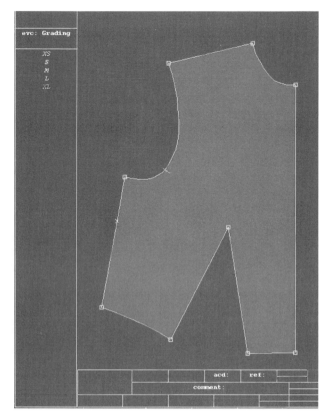

Figure 3.17a Title block with alpha sizing.

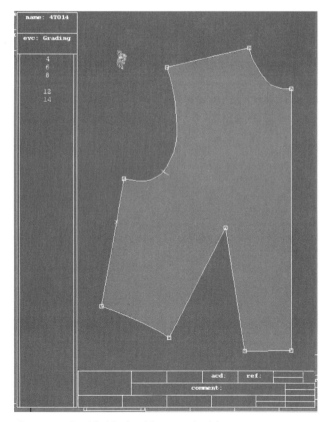

Figure 3.17b Title block with numeric sizing.

Table 3.2 Size Table Symbols

Symbols	Characteristic
*	Marks the base or sample size; placed before the size number
!	Marks break size (average) in alphanumeric tables
2 (the size)	Smallest size number, then the number 2
2 (the size)	2, then mode size

Exercises

1. Calculate curved point placement for an original pattern created manually.

2. Digitize an original pattern created manually.

3. On the CD-ROM, open the file named Pattern Correction Exercise. Identify and correct the problems with the pattern pieces in the file.

4. Create a numeric size table for menswear sizes 32 to 40 and for women's sizes 0 to 18.

5. Create an alpha size table for plus-size women's wear sizes 1X to 4X.

(15 handouts)

Key Terms and Commands

Alpha sizing

Cartesian graph

Curve point

F3>Deletion

F5>Derived Pieces>Sym2Pts

F5>Derived Pieces>Join

Digitizing

F7>Evolution System>Imp.EVT

F7>Evolution System>Rep.EVT

Model sheet

Mouse

Numeric sizing

F1>Points>Add Point

F1>Points> Ali2Pts

F1>Points>Ali3Pts

F3>Point Modification>Reshape

Point Modification>Simplify

Sheet>Arrange all

Sheet>New sheet

Pattern Manipulation

4

Pattern manipulation, including the principles of dart manipulation, added fullness, and contouring, are common practices in the apparel industry. The overall objective of this chapter is to apply traditional flat-pattern techniques using computer applications. Commands commonly used in flat-pattern manipulation are explained, and then applications of the commands are applied to basic flat-pattern techniques. Pattern manipulation is one method of creating patterns in Modaris.

In this chapter, you will learn about the following:

- Commands in Pattern Manipulation
- Bodice Dart Manipulation: Pivoting Darts
- Combining Darts: Bust Dart with Waist Dart
- Dividing Darts: Bust Dart into Two Shoulder Darts
- Dart Caps
- Bodice Seam Lines and Added Fullness
- Darts Equivalent Seam Lines: Princess Seams
- Bodice with Yoke and Added Fullness
- Separating and Joining Back Pattern Pieces
- Adding Skirt Flare
- Lengthening a Pattern
- Adding Pleats
- Contouring: Strapless Bodice
- Key Terms and Commands

Commands in Pattern Manipulation

The following commands are utilized in computer-aided pattern manipulation. The explanation of the commands includes a short description of the command and instructions for activating, implementing, and accepting a procedure or command.

F1>Points>Sliders is used to place a point along an existing line. The point belongs to the line, and you can slide it along the line. A slider point keeps its position proportional in relation to the original line. When you click an existing line, the slider can be permanently placed at that point, or it can slide along the line before being permanently placed. Note: The spacebar selects the adjacent line.

F1>Points>Developed places a point at a specific distance or measurement from another point on the same line. Click a point on a line of a pattern piece, then move the cursor to the new position and click to place the new point.

F1>Points>Relative point places a new point in or on the style relative to the first click or anchor point. Click a point on a line or inside the pattern piece, then move the cursor to the new position and click.

F1>Points>Ali2Pts balances two points along a line to create a straight line. Click one point and then click a second point on a line.

F1>Points>Division adds points automatically at equal intervals when you click two points on a line. A text box appears after you have selected the second point. In the pink area of the text box, type the division number required and then press Enter. The *division number* is the number of line segments required between two points. The number of line segments is one more than the number of points to be added.

F1>Lines>Straight creates a straight line with a beginning and an endpoint. A straight line has only two points. Click to start a line, move the mouse (cursor) to position until the line is the desired length from the opposite end of the line, and click.

After selecting the first endpoint, hold down the Ctrl key on the keyboard. This generates a perfect vertical or horizontal line. Rolling the mouse around the start position in a circular motion allows the line to be created in 45-degree increments.

To create an exact line length, use the text box that opens after the first endpoint is selected. Type the length of the line on the x-axis on the *dx* line of the text box and the length of the line in the y-axis on the *dy* line of the text box. **F1>Lines>Bezier** creates a line that contains both straight and curved segments. Left-click to activate and continue the Bezier line segments. For a curved line segment, hold the Shift key down when left-clicking the segments; release the Shift key to create straight line segments. To undo a line segment, click the right and left mouse buttons simultaneously. Right-click to end the command.

F1>Lines>Semicircular creates a circular line. Left-click to activate, and continue the semicircular line segments. For a curved line segment, hold the Shift key down when left-clicking the segments; release the Shift key to create straight line segments. To undo a line segment, click the right and left mouse buttons simultaneously. Right-click to end the command. The curves of the semicircular lines are rounder than the curved lines created by Bezier lines.

F3>Deletion removes objects, including points and internal lines, from a pattern piece. Note: It does not remove an entire pattern piece from a sheet.

F3>Line modification>Move can be used to move an entire pattern piece or part of a pattern piece to a new location. Select a pattern piece and drag to move an entire pattern piece to a new position. Note: *Move* combined with **F3>Line modification>Stretch** can be used to reposition a group of points or a line segment around a central point. Click the pivot point; then click the point to be moved, reposition the point, and click. Hint: Points may need to be pinned in place before stretching.

F3>Line modification>Lengthen adjusts the length of a curve line between two points. Click two points and a text box appears. The seam length between the points is indicated in the text box. Click in the pink area of the text box, and type in the new seam length by adding the current length, or the amount displayed in the text box, to the additional length required. Lines can also be shortened by this method, except you would subtract the amount to obtain the desired length.

F3>Point modification>Reshape changes the shape of an existing pattern piece. Click a point and move the cursor to the desired position, then click to set the point in the new position.

F3>Point modification>Section creates an endpoint on a line. Click a point to change to an endpoint. Note: An endpoint is usually placed at corners or intersections of lines. Endpoints appear as squares on-screen.

F3>Point modification>Merge changes an endpoint into a regular point called a *characteristic point*. Click the common endpoint to be changed. Hint: If an endpoint is no longer needed, merge the endpoint and then delete the point. Note: Bezier curved lines cannot be merged together.

F3>Point modification>Simplify reduces the number of points between two points along a curved line—for example, to smooth or change the shape of a sleeve cap. Click two points along a curved line; a text box opens. The tolerance appears in the pink area of the text box and is the amount of variation in the line between two points. The user may type in a new amount to adjust.

F3>Point modification>Attach joins two points together into one point. Click a point, move the cursor to a second point, and click to create one point. The first point selected moves to the second point location.

F3>Pins>Pin to hold a part of a pattern piece in place when you are moving a selected group of points or part of a pattern piece. After you have pinned everything that is to be held in place, the unpinned area of the pattern can be moved. Points are pinned. A pinned point appears as a red box.

F3>Pins>Remove Pin unpins all the points on a pattern piece. Click the *Remove Pin* button, and the pins are removed automatically.

F4>Piece>Cut creates a separate pattern piece from an existing pattern piece. Click inside the pattern piece. When the pattern piece turns green, right-click inside the same pattern piece. A new pattern piece is generated.

F5>Derived pieces>Cut Plot cuts a pattern piece apart along an internal line. Click an existing internal line to cut a pattern piece in two pieces. Two new pattern pieces are generated.

F5>Derived pieces>Join combines two pattern pieces into one new pattern piece. On the first piece, click the endpoint of a line and then click the second endpoint of the same line. The pattern piece is now activated. Move the cursor to the second piece and click the two matching endpoints. A new pattern piece is created from the joined components.

F5>Folds>Eff. Fold creation creates a fold on a piece and generates an unfolded pattern piece. Click the start of the fold, the direction of the fold, the width of the fold, and the fold background line. A new pattern piece is generated.

F5>Folds>Pivoting Dart moves a dart to a new location. To pivot the dart, click the dart *apex*, then the endpoint of the fold leg of the dart, then the second dart leg endpoint, and then the predetermined point for placement of the new dart (Figure 4.1). Note: The fold leg of a dart is the leg closest to the front on vertical darts and the lower dart leg on horizontal darts. This folds the darts in the same direction as they are pressed when a garment is constructed. The text box gives you three options for pivoting a dart. The *Ratio* option lets you select the amount of dart to move as a fraction. After you have typed the amount in the pink area of the text box, press Enter. A new pattern piece is created. *DL* option lets you select how much opening, from endpoint to endpoint, of the dart you want to move. *Rotation* option lets you select the amount in terms of the original dart; .5 or ½ moves half of the original dart to the new dart placement.

F5>Folds>Dart Cap creates the end shape of a dart. Click the dart apex, the dart leg endpoint of the fold leg, and then the remaining dart leg endpoint. A new pattern piece is derived.

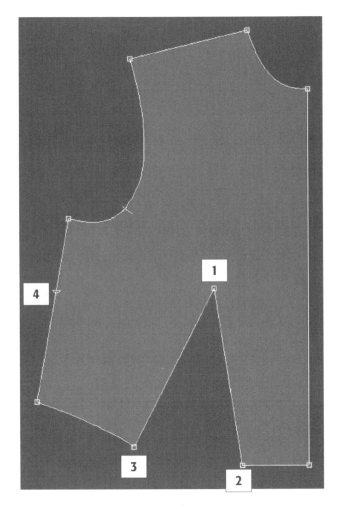

Figure 4.1 Points for pivoting a dart.

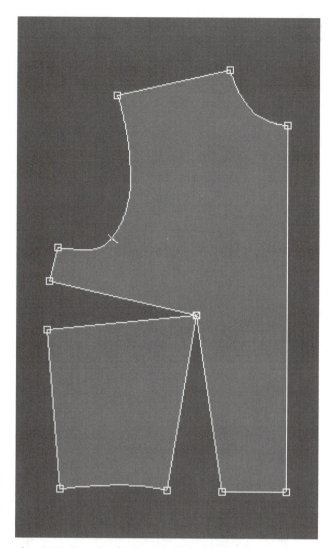

Figure 4.2 Two-dart bodice front with bust and waist darts.

Bodice Dart Manipulation: Pivoting Darts

Fitting **darts** can be moved, combined, or divided into any seam line. The following examples highlight the commands necessary to move, combine, or divide darts using Modaris.

Combining Darts: Bust Dart with the Waist Dart

Combining the Bust Dart with the Waist Dart

1. Digitize a two-dart bodice or open the file named Two-dart Bodice provided on the CD-ROM (Figure 4.2). Hint: Create a copy of the original bodice front using *Sheet>Copy* when the original pattern piece is needed in the design. Click the original bodice front to select, and click to place a new bodice front. To view all the pattern pieces in the file, press the J or the 8 on your keyboard. Right-click to select the pattern piece you want to activate for dart manipulation; then, to view only that pattern piece, press the Home key.

- define pivot pt.
- dart legs

2. Select *F5>Folds>Pivoting Dart* to combine the bust dart with the waist dart. Click the dart apex, the two endpoints of the dart legs, and an endpoint of the waist dart. The *Ratio* text box menu allows a specific amount of the dart to be pivoted (Figure 4.3)—in this case, type "1," since the entire bust dart is to be pivoted. A new pattern piece is generated (Figure 4.4). Hint: If an extra **dart leg** appears, use *F3>Point modification>Attach* and attach the endpoint to the dart apex. Note: Similar steps are used for pivoting and combining darts.

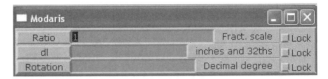

Figure 4.3 Pivoting Dart Ratio text box.

Figure 4.4 One-dart bodice front with waist dart.

Figure 4.5 Division text box.

Figure 4.6 Pivoting a half dart text box.

Figure 4.7 Bodice front with shoulder, bust, and waist dart.

Dividing Darts: Bust Dart into Two Shoulder Darts

Dividing the Bust Dart into Two Darts

1. Digitize a two-dart bodice or open the two-dart bodice file named Two-dart Bodice provided on the CD-ROM (Figure 4.2).

2. The shoulder seam requires points to pivot the darts. To divide the shoulder seam into three line segments, select *F1>Points>Division*. A text box opens; three line segments will add two points to the line, so type "3" in the text box (Figure 4.5). Hint: Check the type of marking selected by clicking on the dog-ear to open the text box with the marking or notch options. If *No Mark* is activated, the second new point and the first dart will disappear after the dart is pivoted. *No Mark* is the default and is indicated by a small white X on-screen. Think of the *No Mark* X as a temporary mark that disappears.

3. Select *F5>Folds>Pivoting dart* to create the first shoulder dart. First, click the dart apex, then the endpoint of the fold leg of the dart, then the second dart leg end-point, and then the point for placement of the new dart. Pivot half the bust dart to the shoulder point to create the first dart by typing "1/2" into the text box (Figure 4.6). A new pattern piece is generated (Figure 4.7).

4. Repeat Step 3 to create the second shoulder dart. Keep in mind, however, that all of the remaining bust dart is pivoted to the second shoulder dart and therefore the ratio is 1. A new pattern piece is generated (Figure 4.8).

5. The dart apexes need to be relocated for the shoulder darts to be parallel. Select *F3>Point modification>Reshape* to move the dart apexes into the pivot circle. Click the dart apex, and drag the dart apex (and dart legs) into the desired position. Hint: Keep the dart apexes in the pivot circle for a good fit. Dart legs must be of equal length.

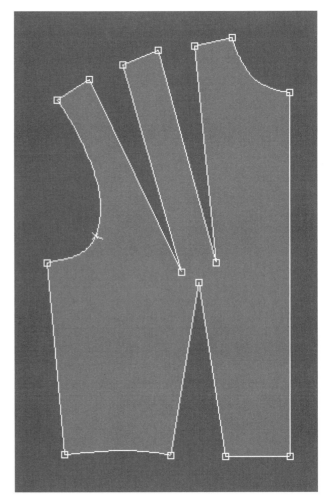

Figure 4.8 Bodice with two parallel shoulder darts and waist dart.

6. After the darts are created and repositioned, you can add new endpoints for the line segments. Select *F3>Point modification>Section* and click the point to be changed. Hint: If apexes are *No Mark,* they will disappear when a new pattern piece is generated.

Dart Caps

Dart caps are the computer's equivalent of a dart shape at the pattern's end when you are creating a pattern by hand. The dart cap is the shape of the open end of a dart. The direction of a dart that you fold by hand should be maintained when you are creating dart caps using the computer.

Creating Dart Caps

1. Digitize a two-dart bodice or open the two-dart bodice file named Two-dart Bodice provided on the CD-ROM (Figure 4.2).

2. Before creating dart caps, change dart apexes from *No Mark.* Select *F1>Points> Relative point* and click the dog-ear to reveal the point types. Do not activate *No Mark* or the apex points will vanish when the new pattern piece is generated.

3. To create dart caps, select *F5>Folds>Dart cap.* Click the dart apex, and then click the two endpoints of the dart. A new pattern piece is generated (Figure 4.9). Repeat this step to create the second dart cap (Figure 4.10).

Bodice Seam Lines and Added Fullness

Bodice design variations can be developed by producing dart-equivalent seam lines or yokes, or by adding fullness. The following examples are for basic princess and yoke seam lines; the same commands can be used to produce many design variations.

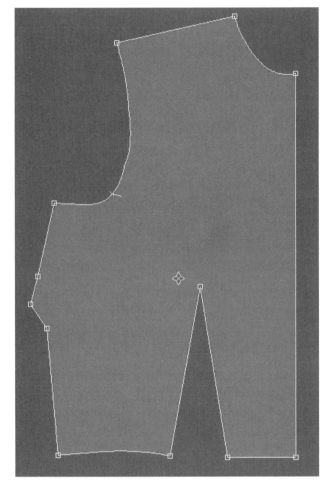

Figure 4.9 Bust dart with dart cap and waist dart without dart cap.

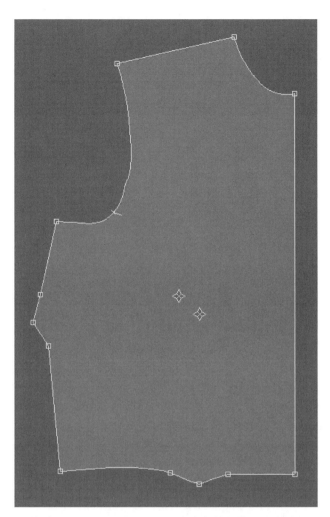

Figure 4.10 Bodice front with bust and waist dart caps.

Dart-Equivalent Seam Lines: Princess Seams

Creating Dart-Equivalent Seams: Princess Seams

1. Digitize a two-dart bodice or open the two-dart bodice file named Two-dart Bodice provided on the CD-ROM (Figure 4.2).

2. The shoulder seam line needs a point to pivot the dart. To place a point in the middle of the shoulder seam line, select *F1>Points>Division*. Divide the seam line into two line segments by clicking each endpoint and dividing by 2.

3. Select *F5>Folds>Pivoting Dart* to pivot the bust dart to the shoulder seam line and pivot the bust dart to the shoulder. A new pattern piece is generated (Figure 4.11).

4. Select *F5>Derived pieces>Cut Plot* to cut the bodice into two pattern pieces: yoke and lower bodice. Click an existing internal line to cut a pattern piece in two pieces. Two new pattern pieces are generated (Figure 4.12). Hint: If only one new pattern piece is generated with Cut Plot, select *F4>Piece>Cut*. Click inside the pattern piece not generated as a new pattern piece. When the pattern piece turns green, right-click inside the pattern piece. The additional pattern piece required is generated.

5. True or smooth the princess seam line by selecting *Display>Curve pts* to display the curved points on the pattern. Select *F3>Point modification>Reshape* to smooth the **bust point**. Hint: You may need to add additional points to the bodice princess seam lines to create a smooth bust point.

6. The new pattern pieces will need the title bar information from the original pattern piece. Select *F4>Industrialisation> Exchange data* and click the title bar of the sheet with the correct information. Then click the title bar of the newly created pattern piece. The information is transferred to the new sheet.

Bodice with Yoke and Added Fullness

Adding Yoke and Bodice Fullness

1. Digitize a two-dart bodice or open the two-dart bodice file named Two-dart Bodice provided on the CD-ROM (Figure 4.2).

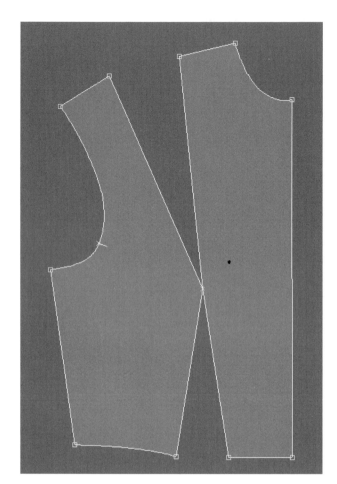

Figure 4.11 Bodice front with shoulder and waist darts.

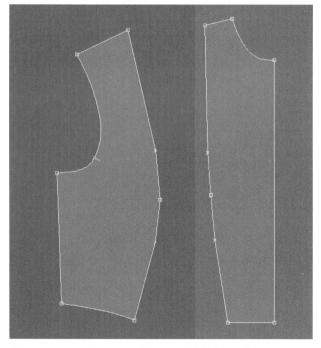

Figure 4.12 Bodice center front and side front pieces.

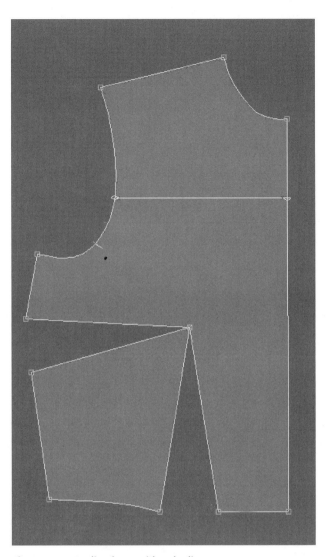

Figure 4.13 Bodice front with yoke line.

2. Using *F1>Points>Developed,* add a point 3″ down from the neckline on the center front seam line to determine the placement of the yoke line. The yoke line is created using *F1>Lines>Straight* to draw a straight line from the developed point from center front to the armhole. To keep the line perpendicular to center front, hold the Shift key down before clicking on the developed point to constrain the axis when creating the line (Figure 4.13).

3. To create two pattern pieces, select *F5>Derived pieces>Cut Plot.* To generate two new pattern pieces and delete the original pattern piece, hold the Shift key down when you select the line to be cut. New pattern pieces are then generated (Figure 4.14). Note: Do not activate Extraction with Dependency in the dialog box. When a pattern piece is extracted with dependency, the two pieces act in tandem—change one and the other piece automatically changes. This can be a problem when you are making additional pattern changes to one of the pattern pieces. Only use Extraction with Dependency when you want to make the same changes to both sides of a pattern. It is generally easier to make all the changes to half the pattern and then create the other half of the pattern piece.

Figure 4.14 Bodice front with yoke.

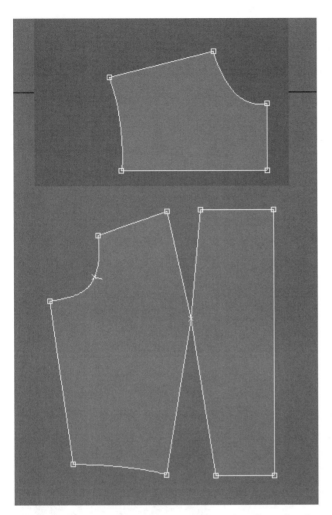

Figure 4.15 Bodice yoke and lower front with yoke and waist darts.

4. Gathers are created by pivoting the bust dart to the yoke seam line. For dart placement, insert a point along the yoke seam line using **F1>Points>Add Point**. Pivot the dart to the yoke line using *F5>Folds> Pivoting dart*. A new pattern piece is generated (Figure 4.15). Hint: If the pattern piece is no longer vertical, select **F2>Orientation>Rot 2pt**. To reposition the pattern piece horizontally, click two points to turn a pattern piece. Select *F2>Orientation>90˚* or *F2>Orientation> 180˚* to rotate the pattern piece into position vertically.

5. *F3>Point modification>Reshape* is used to convert the darts to fullness. Click a dart apex and move it the appropriate seam lines. Repeat for the other dart.

6. For additional fullness, the pattern must first be held in place with *F3>Pins>Pin*. To maintain the yoke curve, add a point along the yoke line $^1/_2''$ from center front and along the waistline $^1/_2''$ from center front. Pin the two new points in place.

7. To add fullness, select *F3>Line modification>Move,* click the bodice center front line, and move until the desired amount of fullness has been added (Figure 4.16).

8. To straighten the side seam, select *F1>Points>Ali2Pts.* Click the underarm/ side seam intersection point and then the waistline/side seam intersection point. In addition to straightening the side seam, this will add additional fullness at the waist.

9. To straighten the waist seam line, activate *Display>Curve pts,* then select *F3>Points> Deletion* to remove curved points. Convert the endpoints using *F3>Point modification>Merge* so that the point can be deleted.

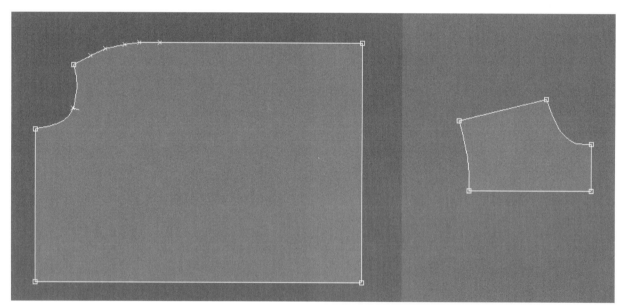

Figure 4.16 Bodice front yoke with added fullness.

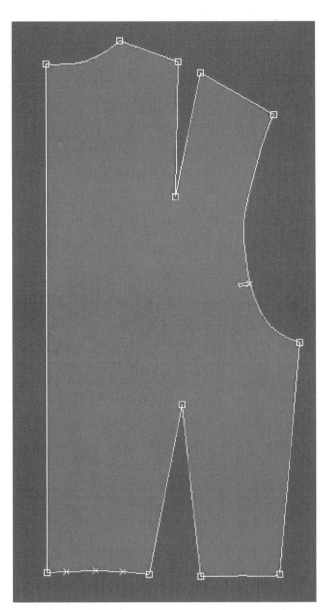

Figure 4.17 Bodice back.

Separating and Joining Back Pattern Pieces

Separating and Joining Back Pattern Pieces

1. Digitize a bodice back or open the back bodice file named Back Bodice provided on the CD-ROM (Figure 4.17).

2. The steps to separate the back into two pieces and create a yoke and lower bodice is similar to creating the yoke front in the previous section, "Bodice with Yoke and Added Fullness." Using *F1>Point> Developed*, add a point 5″ down from the center back/neckline (Figure 4.18).

3. You should pivot the dart to the armhole/ yoke line before cutting the pattern into two pieces. Select *F5>Folds>Pivoting Dart* to pivot the dart to the armhole at the height desired for the yoke line. Type "1" in the text box to pivot the entire shoulder dart (Figure 4.19). The point from the dart will remain after the dart is pivoted. To eliminate the point, select *F3>Point modification>Merge*, then select *Deletion* to remove the shoulder point.

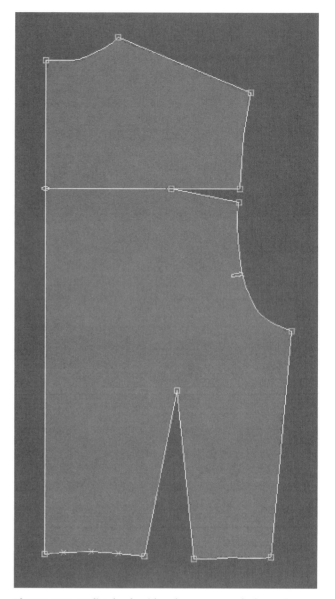

Figure 4.18 Bodice back with yoke seam, armhole, and waist darts.

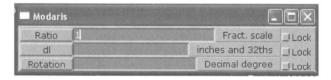

Figure 4.19 Pivoting a dart text box.

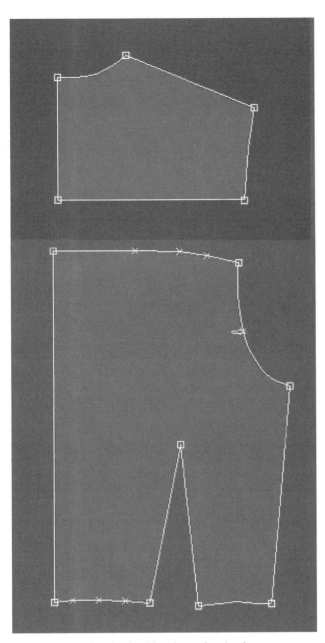

Figure 4.20 Bodice back with yoke and waist darts.

4. To create two pattern pieces, select *F5>Derived pieces>Cut2Pts.* Two new pattern pieces are derived (Figure 4.20). Note: Do not activate Extraction with Dependency. Hint: If two pieces are not derived, select *F4>Piece>Cut* to obtain the missing piece.

5. To join the back yoke and lower back, press the End key on the keyboard and move the yoke above the lower-back pattern piece.

6. Zoom closer to include only the two pattern pieces on-screen. Hint: The middle zoom button can be used to create a box around the two pattern pieces.

7. Select *F5>Derived pieces>Join.* Figure 4.21 indicates the order in which to click the endpoints to join two pattern pieces together. After the first two points have been selected, the yoke will be activated. It can then be moved closer to the lower back.

Adding Skirt Flare

Maintaining the Waist Dart and Adding Flare

1. Digitize a skirt or open the basic skirt file named One-dart Skirt provided on the CD-ROM (Figure 4.22).

2. To hold the skirt in place for flaring, select *F3>Pins>Pin.* Pin the center front/hemline intersecting point and the side seam/waistline intersecting point.

3. To flare the side seam, select *F3>Line modification>Stretch.* Click the hip point side seam, which acts as a pivot point, and then select the side seam/hemline intersection point and rotate to create the flare (Figure 4.23). The text box indicates the amount of flare that has been added (Figure 4.24).

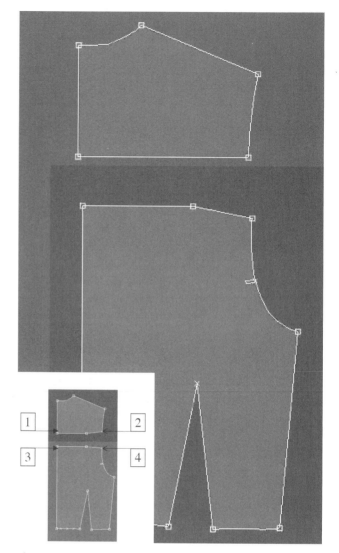

Figure 4.21 Points for joining two pattern pieces.

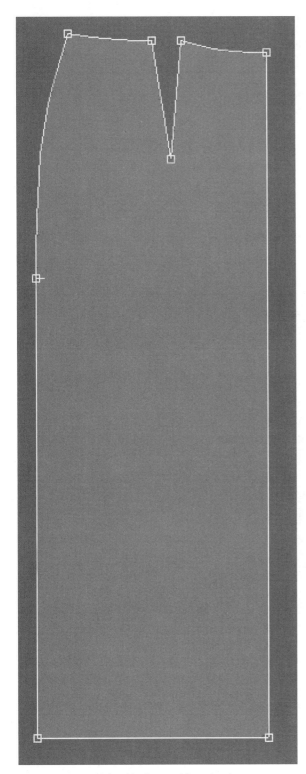

Figure 4.22 Straight skirt front with waist dart.

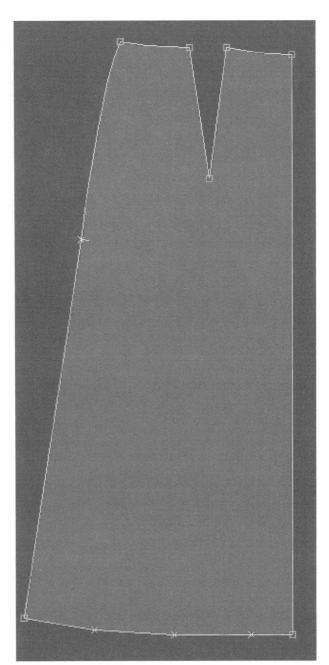

Figure 4.23 Straight skirt, adding flare.

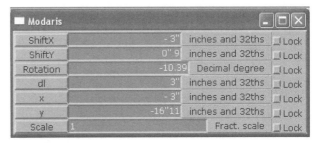

Figure 4.24 Stretch text box.

4. Select *F3>Pin>Remove Pin* to remove all the pins on the sheet.

5. The hemline will be straight when the flare is added (Figure 4.25).

6. Use *F1>Points>Division* to add three points to the hemline. The number of line segments is entered into the text box; therefore, four line segments are required for three points (Figure 4.26).

7. To curve the hemline, select *F3>Point modification>Reshape*, then click and move points until a smooth curved hem is created (Figure 4.27).

Pivoting the Waist Dart to Create Flare

A second option for adding flare is when the waist dart is not maintained. Then the dart is pivoted into the hem (Figure 4.28).

1. Add a point at the hem, *F1>Points>Division*.

2. Pivot the dart to the new point created at the hem, *F5>Folds>Pivoting Darts*.

3. Select *F3>Point modification>Reshape*, click the dart endpoint, and drag the dart endpoint down to the hemline. Additional points may be required to create a smooth curve to the hem.

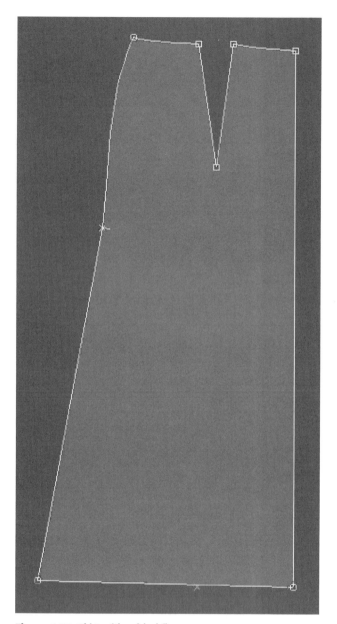

Figure 4.25 Skirt with added flare.

Figure 4.26 Division text box.

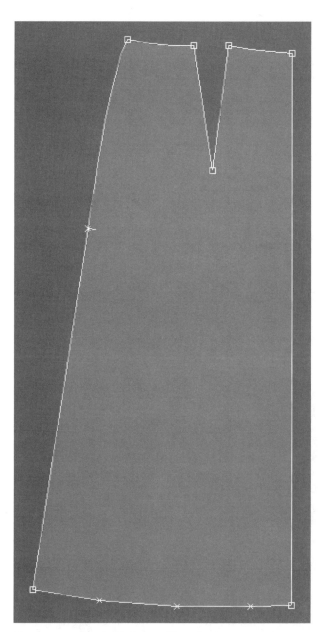

Figure 4.27 Flared skirt front with waist dart.

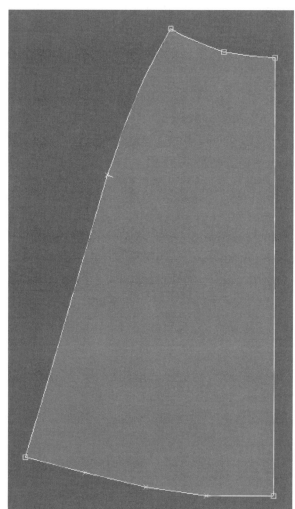

Figure 4.28 Flared skirt front with no waist dart.

Lengthening a Pattern

The two methods for lengthening patterns are presented. The first is for lengthening an area, such as lengthening the hem on the torso block to create a dress block. The command *Move* can be used for straight seams such as hems, pleats, and extensions, including button closures. The second method of lengthening is using a curved seam line, such as the sleeve cap, to create gathers or a puff sleeve. In lengthening a sleeve, it is important to maintain the sleeve cap length below the notches and add the fullness above the notches. This allows the sleeve to fit the bodice and gathers to be correctly placed and not under the arm.

Lengthening a Torso

1. Digitize a torso or open the torso block file named Torso Block provided on the CD-ROM (Figure 4.29).

2. *Select F3>Pin>Pin* to hold the torso in place at the waist/side seam and center front/neckline intersection.

3. To lengthen the torso 10″, select *F3>Line modification>Move* and click in the center of the hem. A text box opens; type "10″" on the *dl* (distance length) line (Figure 4.30).

4. Click to place the new hem (Figure 4.31). Hint: When *Print* is activated on the status bar, both the original hemline (purple) and the new hemline (white) can be viewed.

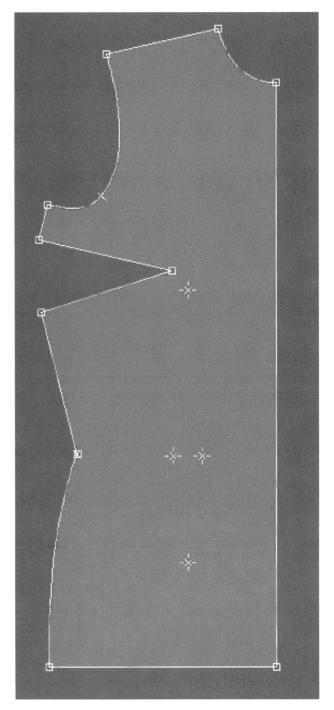

Figure 4.29 Torso front.

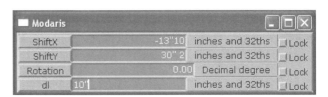

Figure 4.30 Move text box.

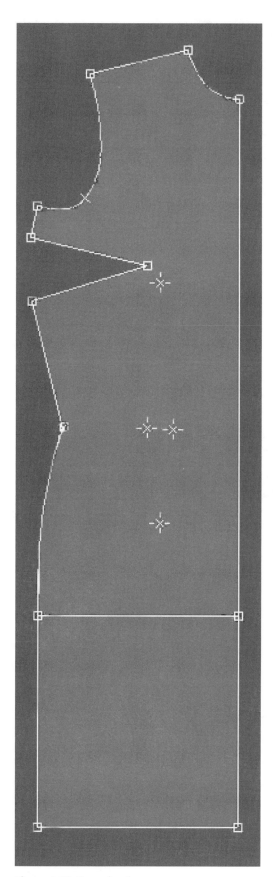

Figure 4.31 Dress front.

Lengthening a Sleeve Capline or Curved Seam

1. Digitize a sleeve or open the sleeve file named Sleeve Block provided on the CD-ROM (Figure 4.32). Hint: To keep the original sleeve, select *Sheet>Copy* and right-click to place the new pattern piece. Keeping the original pattern piece is important when you are trying new commands or the pattern work does not generate a new pattern piece.

2. Select *F1>Lines>Straight* and draw two straight lines from the front and back notches to the wrist/underarm seam intersection point (Figure 4.33).

3. Separate the sleeve into three pattern pieces using *F5>Derived pieces>Cut Plot* or *F4>Industrialisation>Cut* (Figure 4.34). Dividing the sleeve into three pieces allows lengthening of the sleeve cap.

4. To lengthen piece 2, the center piece, place notches 4″ up from the notches on either side. Select *F3>Pins>Pin* and pin the new points and the waist/underarm intersection points.

5. Select *F3>Line modification>Move,* click the cap/intersection point, and drag the point 1½″ or the amount of one-half the desired fullness. Click the second cap/intersection point and drag the point 1½″ or the amount of one-half the desired fullness (Figure 4.35). *Print* can help you see the change in the pattern piece. The *Move* text box can also be used to acquire the desired amount of fullness; type in the amount to add on the *dl* line or the total length on the *Length* line (Figure 4.36).

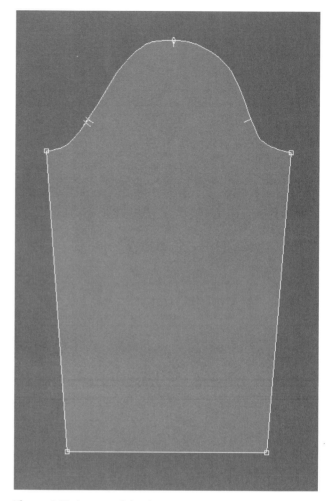

Figure 4.32 Long straight sleeve.

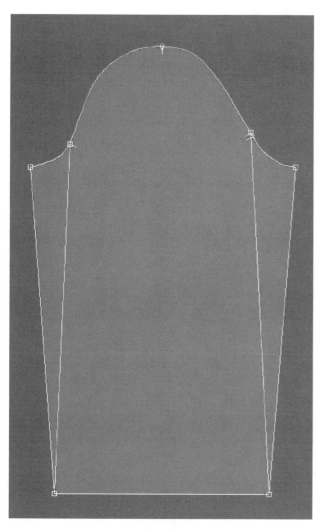

Figure 4.33 Long sleeve with split lines.

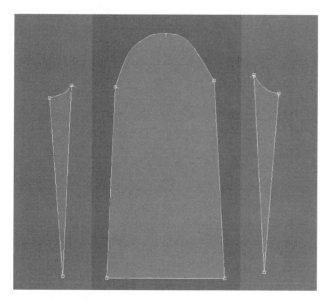

Figure 4.34 Three sleeve pieces.

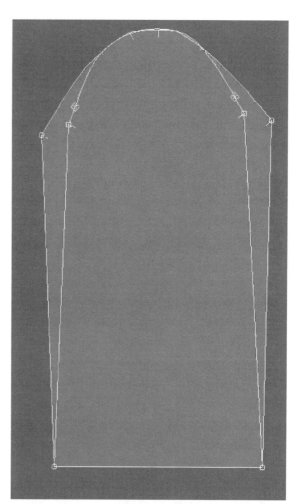

Figure 4.35 Lengthened center pieces with join points.

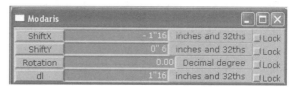

■ Modaris			□□☒
ShiftX	– 1"16	inches and 32ths	⌐Lock
ShiftY	0" 6	inches and 32ths	⌐Lock
Rotation	0.00	Decimal degree	⌐Lock
dl	1"16	inches and 32ths	⌐Lock

Figure 4.36 Move text box.

6. Select *F5>Derived pieces>Join* to reconnect the three sleeve pieces back together. After the first two points of one underarm piece have been selected, the back underarm sleeve piece will be activated; move it to point 3 of the upper sleeve. Repeat to attach the front underarm sleeve piece to the upper sleeve using *F3>Point modification>Reshape* to true or smooth the sleeve cap (Figure 4.37). Hint: Remember to zoom in and out when trueing.

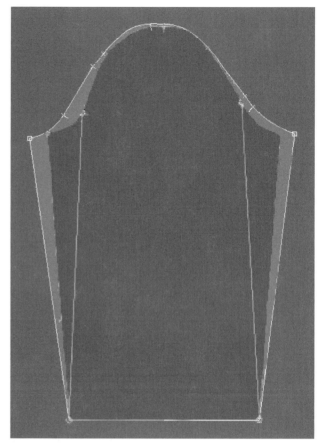

Figure 4.37 Sleeve with lengthened cap.

Figure 4.38 Lengthen text box.

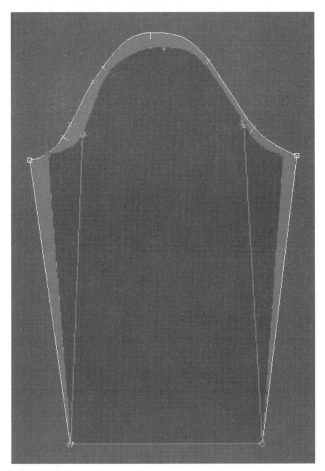

Figure 4.39 Long sleeve with cap fullness for gathers.

7. If the sleeve cap height is not raised enough, select *F3>Line modification> Lengthen*. Click the points previously added to control the placement of the gathers. After the second click, the text box opens. In the *dl* line, type "1″" or the desired amount the cap is to be raised (Figure 4.38). The old length of the sleeve plus the gather length can be added together and typed in the *Length* line of the text box. Only lengthen above the sleeve notches. Hint: If *Lengthen* is only used to increase the length of the sleeve cap, it will raise the cap but not add fullness to the sleeve circumference. Sleeve circumference fullness is also desired when the sleeve cap is raised (Figure 4.39).

Adding Pleats

Pleats can be added on a bodice, skirt, or sleeves. The method for adding pleats remains the same regardless of the body placement.

Creating a Center Front Pleat

1. Digitize a one-dart bodice or open the one-dart bodice file named One-dart Bodice provided on the CD-ROM (Figure 4.4).

2. Select *F5>Folds>Eff. Fold creation*, and click to create the pleat as indicated in Figure 4.40. After the first click, the cursor is activated and a text box appears indicating the width of the pleat (Figure 4.41).

3. The cursor is still activated. Move the cursor to identify the background line of the pleat. A new pattern piece is generated (Figure 4.42). Hint: *F5>Folds>Eff. Fold creation* can also be used to add fullness to a pattern piece. The beginning and end of the pleat can be the width added to a pattern piece such as a sleeve with gathers at the wrist.

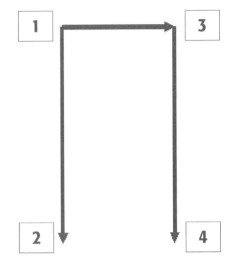

Figure 4.40 Steps for pleat creation.

Figure 4.41 Pleat creation text box.

Figure 4.42 Bodice front with center front pleat.

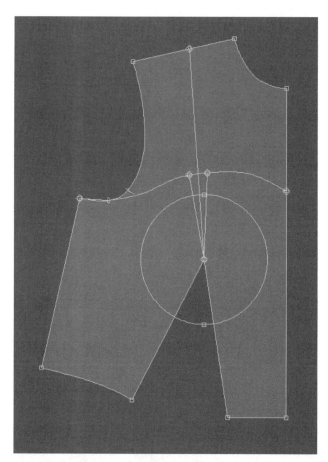

Figure 4.43 Strapless corset front style lines.

Contouring: Strapless Bodice

Contouring

When the garment design requires closer fitting than a basic garment, contouring is required. Contoured designs include strapless, sleeveless garments, lowered necklines, empire styles, and bra-style tops. While contouring is necessary for a variety of design styles, the commands necessary for contouring are similar. Contouring is done to create a close fit. The following commands allow for a closer fit to the upper torso than does the basic garment (Armstrong, 2005).

Contouring Strapless Design

1. Digitize a one-dart bodice or open the one-dart bodice file named One-dart Bodice provided on the CD-ROM (Figure 4.4).

2. To add a **bust circle**, select **F2>Tools>Circle** and create a circle 4″ in diameter (Figure 4.43). Click the bust apex and drag the cursor, or type the amount in the text box.

3. The shoulder seam line requires a point for pivoting the dart. Select *F1>Points>Division* to divide the seam line into two line segments.

4. Draw a line from the bust apex to the midpoint of the shoulder seam with *F1>Line>Straight.*

5. Create the strapless bodice style line by using *F1>Line>Bezier* from the side seam/underarm intersection, above the bust circle, and ending at center front.

6. Using *F1>Points>Relative point,* add two relative points, along the strapless bodice style line $^{14}/_{32}$″ to the right and $^{14}/_{32}$″ to the left of the princess line/style line intersection.

7. Connect the bust point with the two points created in Step 6 using *F1>Line>Straight.*

8. To remove excess **ease** above the bust, select *F4>Piece>Cut,* left-click the center front panel and left-click the bust circle, then right-click to end the command. Repeat the procedure with the side front and bust circle. New pattern pieces are derived (Figure 4.44). Go to Step 10 if your design has princess seam lines. Note: If the center front and side front are not joined, the side front must be reshaped or trued.

9. Join the center front and side front panels to create a single front pattern piece by selecting *F5>Derived pieces>Join.* The new pattern piece will be $^{28}/_{32}''$ shorter along the style line.

10. To contour at the side seam, add a point *F1>Point>Add Point* $^1/_2''$ down from the side seam/underarm intersection and a point $^1/_2''$ along the style line from the underarm/side seam intersection.

11. To remove the excess ease, select *F3>Point modification>Attach.* Connect the underarm/side seam intersection with the point along the side seam created in Step 10. Attach that point to the point along the style line created in Step 10.

12. To contour between the bust, select *F1>Line>Straight* and draw a line perpendicular with center front.

13. Add one point $^{12}/_{32}''$ above and $^{12}/_{32}''$ below the line created in Step 11. Using a straight line, connect the bust apex with the points.

14. Use *F4>Piece>Cut* to cut the center front piece above the new line. Cut the center front piece below the new line. Two new pattern pieces are generated.

15. Join the two pieces using *F5>Derived piece>Join* to create the new front piece. A new pattern piece is generated (Figure 4.45).

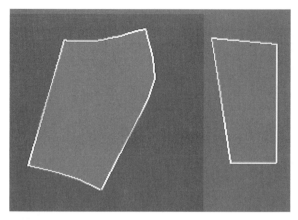

Figure 4.44 Strapless corset front with princess lines.

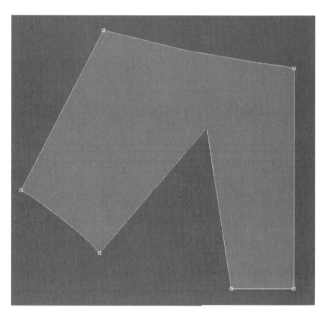

Figure 4.45 One-piece strapless corset front.

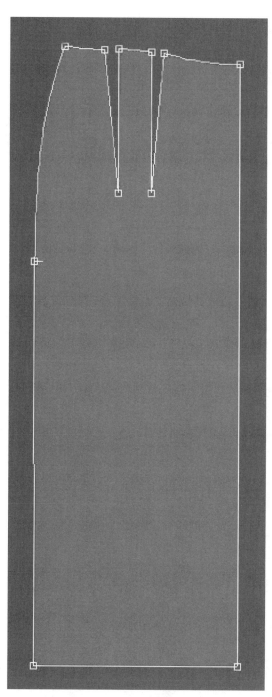

Figure 4.46 Two-dart skirt front.

Exercises

The following exercises are to provide additional applications and review of the key commands related to pattern manipulation including dart manipulation and added fullness.

Exercise 1: Pivoting Basic Skirt Darts

1. Digitize a skirt block or open the skirt file named Two-dart Skirt Block provided on the CD-ROM (Figure 4.46).

2. On the skirt front, extend the dart end-points to the skirt pivot points; $1\frac{1}{2}''$ below the dart endpoint is the basic pivot point, using *F1>Lines>Straight*. You can also extend the dart down $1\frac{1}{2}''$ by using *F3>Point modification>Reshape* and dragging the dart endpoint. A text box opens indicating the dl, which represents the length that the endpoint of a line has been moved (Figure 4.47).

3. Select *F5>Folds>Pivoting Dart* and pivot the first waist dart to the center front/waist intersection point of the skirt. A new pattern piece is generated (Figure 4.48).

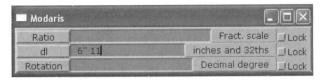

Figure 4.47 Text box showing the dl.

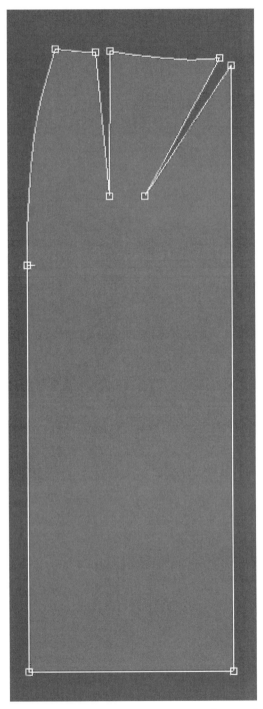

Figure 4.48 Two-dart skirt with waist and center front darts.

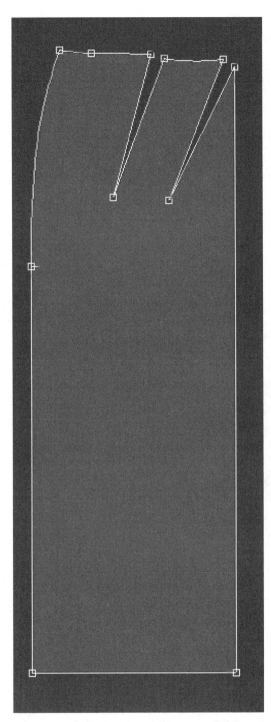

Figure 4.49 Two-dart skirt with two parallel darts.

4. Select *F5>Folds>Pivoting Dart* and pivot the second dart to the first waist dart's original placement along the waist of the skirt. Using *F1>Points>Developed*, you can add a point along the waistline for pivoting the dart. A new pattern piece is generated (Figure 4.49).

5. Select *F3>Point modification>Reshape* to move the dart legs parallel to each other and for the dart legs to be the same length. Hint: A parallel line can be used to check the dart legs.

6. The dart ends should be endpoints or type 2 points; select *F3>Point modification> Section* to change the point types at the end of the dart legs.

7. Select *F5>Folds>Dart cap* to create the dart caps. A new pattern piece is generated.

8. If the pattern piece is no longer vertical, select *F2>Orientation>Rotate 2pt* to first orientate the piece horizontally, and then select *F2>Orientation>-90* to orient the piece vertically.

Exercise 2: Combining Darts

Moving the bust and the waist dart to the neckline/center front is another example of combining two darts into one.

1. Digitize a two-dart bodice or open the two-dart bodice file named Two-dart Bodice provided on the CD-ROM (Figure 4.2).

2. Select *F5>Folds>Pivoting Dart* to combine the waist dart with the bust dart. Click the waist dart apex, the two endpoints of the waist dart legs, and an endpoint of the bust dart. The *Ratio* text box menu item allows a specific amount of the dart to be pivoted. In this case, type "1," since the entire waist dart is to be pivoted into the bust dart (Figure 4.50). A new pattern piece is generated (Figure 4.51).

3. Select *F5>Folds>Dart cap* to create the dart cap; click the dart apex, then the two endpoints of the dart. A new pattern piece is generated.

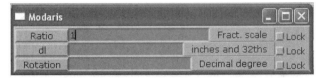

Figure 4.50 Pivoting a dart text box.

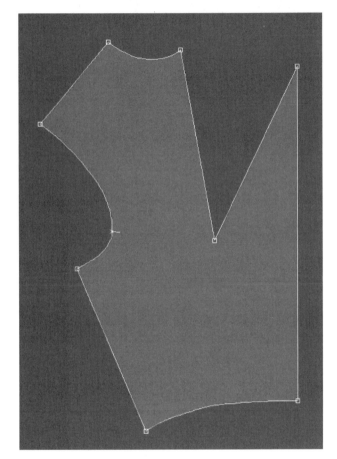

Figure 4.51 Bodice front with neckline dart.

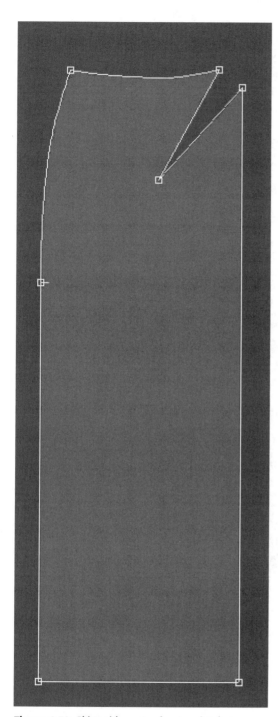

Figure 4.52 Skirt with center front waist dart.

Exercise 3: Combining Skirt Darts

1. Digitize a skirt block or open the skirt file named Two-dart Skirt Block provided on the CD-ROM (Figure 4.46).

2. Extend the dart endpoints to the skirt pivot points; $1\frac{1}{2}''$ below the dart endpoint is the basic pivot point.

3. Select *F5>Folds>Pivoting Dart* and pivot the two waist darts to the center front / waist intersection point of the skirt. A new pattern piece is generated (Figure 4.52).

4. Select *F5>Folds>Dart cap* to create the dart cap. A new pattern piece is generated.

Exercise 4: Dividing Darts

Pivoting the bust dart into two neckline darts is an example of dividing a dart. Digitize a two-dart bodice or open the two-dart bodice file named Two-dart Bodice provided on the CD-ROM (Figure 4.2).

1. Select *F5>Folds>Pivoting Dart* to create the first neckline dart at the center front seam. Pivot half the bust dart to the shoulder point to create the first dart by typing "1/2" into the text box (Figure 4.53). A new pattern piece is generated (Figure 4.54).

2. The neckline seam requires a point to create the second dart. Select *F1>Points> Add Point* and place a point 1″ from the center front/neckline.

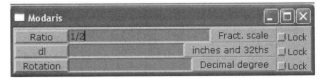

Figure 4.53 Pivoting a dart text box.

Figure 4.54 Bodice front with half bust dart pivoted to the neckline.

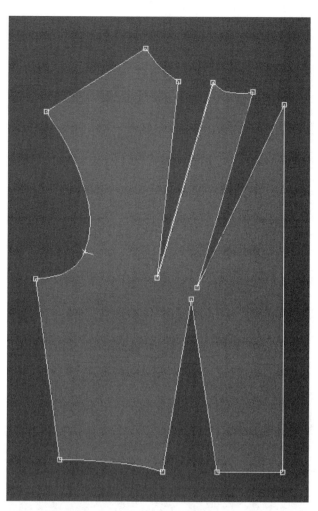

Figure 4.55 Bodice front with two parallel neckline darts and waist dart.

3. Repeat Step 2 to create the second neckline dart, pivoting all the remaining bust darts to the neckline. A new pattern piece is generated (Figure 4.55).

4. Relocate the shoulder darts parallel to the center front neckline dart. Select *F3>Point modification>Reshape* to move the dart apexes into the pivot circle. Click the dart apex and drag the dart apex (and dart legs) into the desired position. Select **F3>Line modification>Merge** to delete the side seam point.

5. Select *F5>Folds>Dart cap* to create the dart caps. Click the dart apex, then the two endpoints of one dart. A new pattern piece is generated.

6. Repeat Step 5 to create the remaining dart cap.

Exercise 5: Curved Princess Seamlines

A curved princess seam is another version of the princess seam line that originates at the **armscye**, continues through the apex, and extends to the waist.

1. Digitize a two-dart bodice or open the two-dart bodice file named Two-dart Bodice provided on the CD-ROM (Figure 4.2).

2. The armhole seam line needs a point to pivot the dart. Place a point one-third of the distance down from the armhole/shoulder seam intersection; then select *F1>Points>Developed*. Hint: Use *F8>Measurement>Length* to obtain the armhole length.

3. Select *F1>Line>Bezier* to draw a line from the armhole point through the apex to the waist dart (Figure 4.56). Hint: *F3>Line modification>Reshape* can be used to adjust the shape of the princess seam line.

Figure 4.56 Bodice front with princess Bezier line.

Figure 4.57 Curved princess seam line with bust dart.

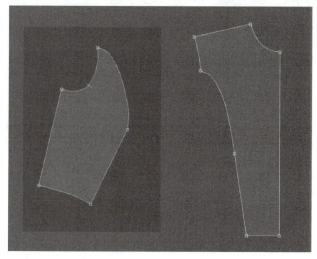

Figure 4.58 Curved princess seam line.

4. Select *F4>Piece>Cut* to cut the bodice into two pattern pieces: yoke or upper and lower front. Click an existing internal line to cut a pattern piece in two pieces. Two new pattern pieces are generated (Figure 4.57).

5. Select *F3>Pins>Pin* and click the dart end and the apex of the dart. This will hold part of the side bodice in place while you are closing the bust dart. Select *F3>Line modification>Stretch* and click the apex of the dart as the pivot point and the dart end that was not pinned. Move the cursor to close the dart (Figure 4.58).

6. True or smooth the princess seam line by selecting *Display>Curve pts* to display the curved points on the pattern. Select *F3>Point modification>Reshape* to smooth the bust point. Hint: When reshaping, select *Display>Curve points.* Additional points may be needed to smooth the bust point. *F3>Point modification>Attach* can be used to remove the bust line and *F3>Point modification>Merge* to remove the remaining bust point on the side seam.

Exercise 6: Midriff Yoke

The midriff yoke is created by creating a horizontal seam line below the bust.

1. Digitize a one-dart bodice or open the one-dart bodice file named One-dart Bodice provided on the CD-ROM (Figure 4.4).

2. Using *F1>Points>Developed,* add a point 4″ up from the waistline on the center front seam line to determine the placement of the yoke line. Place a second point 4″ up from the waist on the side seam. Place a third point and a fourth point 4″ up from the waist (1″ below the bust circle) on the two dart legs. Use *F1>Lines<Bezier* to create a yoke line, drawing a curved line section from the side seam to the bust point and a straight line section from the bust to the developed point at center front (Figure 4.59). Hint: Hold the Shift key down when a curved section of line is desired.

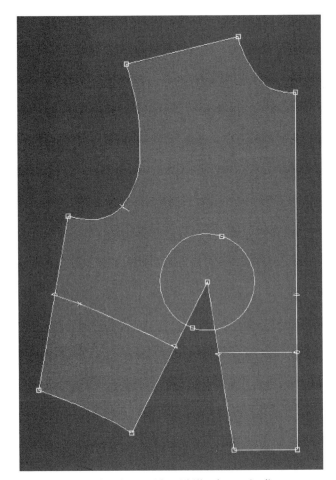

Figure 4.59 Bodice front with midriff yoke Bezier line.

Figure 4.60 Bodice front with two-piece midriff yoke.

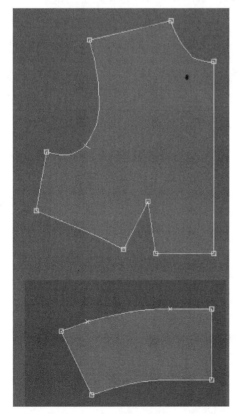

Figure 4.61 Bodice front with one-piece midriff yoke.

3. To create three pattern pieces, select *F4>Piece>Cut.* To generate three new pattern pieces, left-click inside one of the three new pieces. Right-click to cut one piece apart; repeat to cut the remaining two pieces. New pattern pieces are then generated (Figure 4.60).

4. To join the lower center front and the lower side front pattern pieces, press the End key on the keyboard and move the pieces closer together. Select *F5>Derived pieces>Join* to join two pattern pieces together (Figure 4.61).

5. To smooth the midriff yoke seam and waistline, select *F3>Point modification> Reshape.* To create the desired shape, additional curve points may need to be added.

Exercise 7: Added Neckline Fullness

The following is dart equivalent plus added fullness gathers.

1. Digitize a one-dart bodice or open the one-dart bodice file named One-dart Bodice provided on the CD-ROM (Figure 4.4).

2. Using *F1>Points>Developed,* add a point, 1½″ from the center front along the neckline seam.

3. Pivot the waist dart to the neckline point by using *F5>Folds>Pivoting Dart.*

4. Gathers are created by pivoting the waist dart to the neckline seam. Select *F5>Folds>Pivoting Dart* to pivot the waist dart to the neckline point. A new pattern piece is generated (Figure 4.62).

5. To add fullness at the neckline, select *F3>Pins>Pin.* Pin the neckline developed point and the waistline/side seam intersection point.

6. Select *F3>Line modification>Stretch,* click the waistline/center front and the center front/neckline, and move the neckline until the desired amount of fullness has been added (Figure 4.63). Note: The text box indicates the amount of fullness added—in the example, 2″ (Figure 4.64).

7. *F3>Point modification>Reshape* is used to convert the dart to fullness and smooth the neckline. Click a dart apex and move it to the appropriate seam lines at the neckline (Figure 4.65).

Figure 4.62 Bodice front with neckline dart.

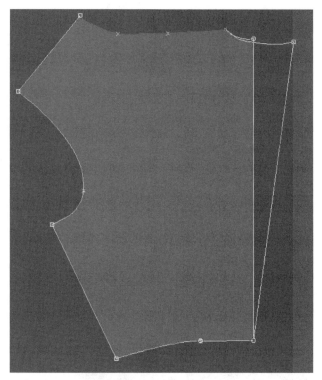

Figure 4.63 Bodice front with stretch.

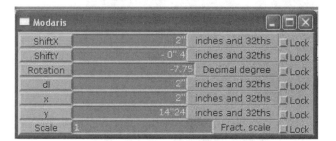

Figure 4.64 Stretch text box.

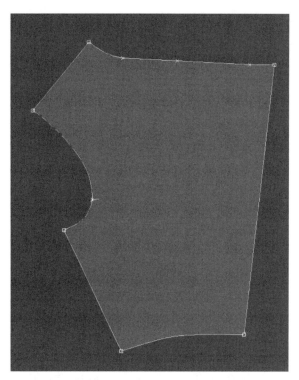

Figure 4.65 Bodice front with added neckline fullness.

Exercise 8: Panel Skirt with Added Flare

Add panels to a skirt to create a six-gore skirt, and then add flare to the gores. The six-gore skirt is developed by cutting panels in the skirt to create a center front panel and a side front panel.

1. Digitize a skirt front or open the skirt front file named Two-dart Skirt Block provided on the CD-ROM (Figure 4.46).

2. Select *F1>Lines>Straight* to draw a straight line down from the dart closest to the center front (Figure 4.66).

3. To create two pattern pieces, select *F5>Derived pieces>Cut Plot* on the panel line created in Step 1 (Figure 4.67).

4. To add a flare line, select *F3>Pins>Pin*. Pin the princess line dart apex and the side seam/hemline intersection point. For the center front pattern piece, pin the princess line dart apex and the center front/hemline intersecting point.

5. To flare the side seam, select *F3>Line modification>Stretch*. Click the hip point side seam, which acts as a pivot point, and then select the side seam/hemline intersection point and rotate to create the flare. Spread the panels 1″ each (Figure 4.68). The text box indicates the amount of flare added (Figure 4.69).

6. Select *F3>Pins>Remove Pin* to remove the pins.

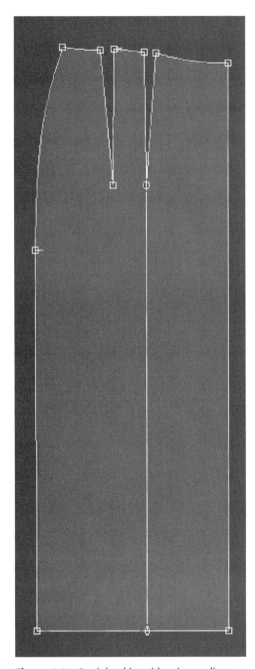

Figure 4.66 Straight skirt with princess line.

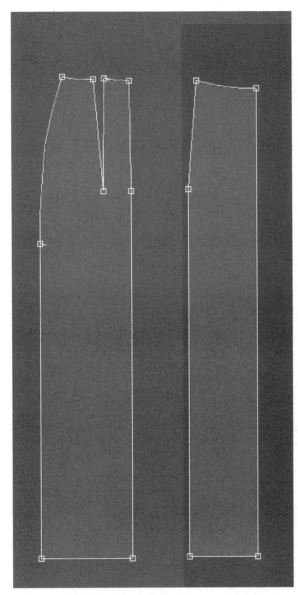

Figure 4.67 Six-gore skirt front.

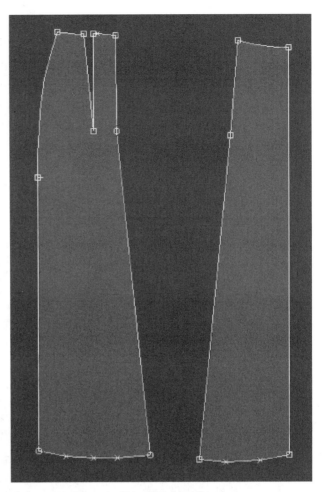

Figure 4.68 Six-gore skirt with added flare.

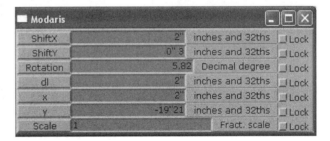

Figure 4.69 Stretch text box.

To true the hem, select *F1>Points>Add Point* and add 3 points equal distance apart along the hem of each pattern piece. Select *F3>Line modification>Reshape,* and click and move points until smooth curved hems are created; additional curve points may need to be added. Hint: How to check the hem shape? Select *F8>Assembly>Marry* and click one point of the center front skirt and the matching point of the side front skirt. The two pieces will be temporarily attached together for checking the hem shape (Figure 4.70). Pieces can be reshaped when they are married. Chapter 6 goes further into checking pattern pieces.

Figure 4.70 Married center front and side front.

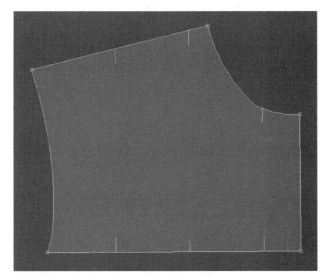

Figure 4.71 Bodice front yoke with notches.

Exercise 9: Bodice Yoke with Pleats

1. Copy the yoke created in the "Bodice with Yoke and Added Fullness" exercise in this chapter without adding fullness to the body.

2. Pleats will be located at 1″, 3″, and 5″ from center front. The points do not remain when a new pattern piece is developed; therefore, after points are added, **notches** should be placed. Notches will be maintained when new pattern pieces are generated. The following instructions are for adding each pleat individually to each new pattern piece that is generated after a pleat has been added, as well as the notches that relate to each pleat. All three pleats can be added and then the notches can be added to indicate the outer fold, inner fold, and matching line of each pleat.

3. *Use F1>Points>Developed* to place a point 1″ from center front along the yoke line (Figure 4.71). Add notches at the yoke and neckline by using *F2>Notches>Notch*.

4. Select *F5>Folds>Eff. Fold creation* and click the starting point of one point to place a pleat fold line. After the first click, the cursor is activated and can be stretched in the fold line direction. Click to identify the end of the fold line. The text box indicates the width of the pleat at the beginning and end of the line (Figure 4.72); 1″ indicates that the pleat will be 1″ deep. Add the notches to indicate the pleat outer fold, inner fold, and matching line by using *F2>Notches>Notch* (Figure 4.73). The fourth point generated is not traditionally indicated but identifies the matching point of the inner fold line of a pleat. You will need to orient notches along the neckline and shoulder line by using *F2>Notches> Orientation.* Zoom in to orient notches. Hint: Before starting the pleating process, check that your yoke line is straight and on grain by using *F1>Orientation>Rot 2 pts.* Also, the center front line should be perpendicular to the yoke line; use *F1>Points> Ali2Pts* to check. Recheck after each pleat is added, and add the required notches.

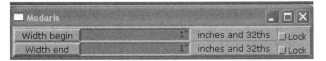

Figure 4.72 Eff. fold creation text box.

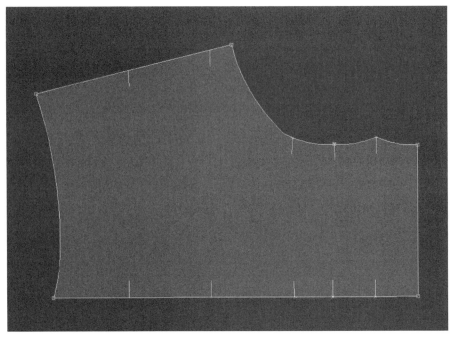

Figure 4.73 Yoke with one pleat.

5. Repeat Step 4 to create the second pleat. Add notches for the second pleat (Figure 4.74).

6. Repeat Step 4 to create the third pleat. Add notches for the third pleat (Figure 4.75).

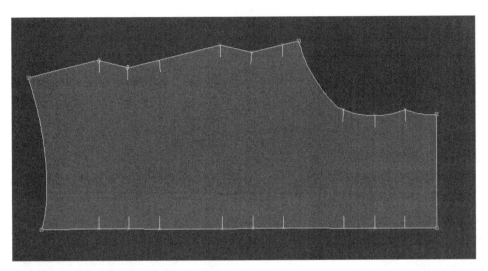

Figure 4.74 Yoke with two pleats.

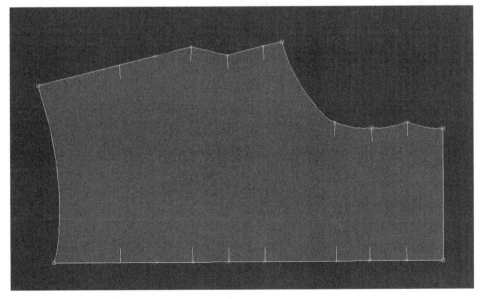

Figure 4.75 Yoke with three pleats.

Key Terms and Commands

armscye

bust circle

Darts

Dart caps

Dart legs

F5>Derived pieces>Cut Plot

F5>Derived pieces>Join

ease

F5>Folds>Dart cap

F5>Folds>Eff. Fold creation

F5>Folds>Pivoting Dart

F3>Line modification>Lengthen

F3>Line modification>Merge

F3>Line modification>Move

F3>Line modification>Stretch

F1>Lines>Bezier

F1>Lines>Straight

F1>Lines>Semicircular

notches

F2>Orientation>Rot 2pt

F4>Piece>Cut

F3>Pins>Pin

F3>Pins>Remove Pin

F3>Point modification>Attach

F3>Point modification>Reshape

F1>Points>Add Point

F1>Points>Ali2Pts

F1>Points>Developed

F1>Points>Division

F1>Points>Relative point

F1>Points>Slider

F2>Tools>Circle

Pattern Creation

5

In this chapter, the commands introduced in Chapter 2 are applied to facings, as well as to drafting or creating pattern pieces on-screen. Drafting or creating pattern pieces on-screen is a technique that can be used to create any pattern pieces, including waistbands, collars, cuffs, pockets, and circular skirts.

In this chapter, you will learn about the following:

- Commands in Pattern Creation
- Creating a Left from a Right Front
- Turn-Back Facing or Attached Facing
- Separate Front Facing
- Back Neck Facing
- Sleeveless Bodice and Armhole Facing
- Drafting
- Circle Skirt
- Collars
- Importing a Model
- Key Terms and Commands

Commands in Pattern Creation

F1>Points>Developed places a point at a particular measurement. Click a point on a line of a pattern piece, then move the cursor to the new position and click.

F1>Points>Add Point adds a characteristic point or a curve point at a relative distance from a reference or point. Click a point, then move the cursor to a new position and click.

F1>Points>Relative point places a new point in or on the style relative to the first click or anchor point. Click a point on a line or inside the pattern piece, and then move the cursor to the new position and click.

F1>Lines>Parallel creates a line parallel to an existing or reference line. Click the reference line, and then move the cursor to the position of the new or parallel line and left-click to place the line.

F1>Lines>Bezier creates a line that contains both straight and curved segments. Left-click to activate and continue the Bezier line segments. For curved line segments, hold the Shift button down when left-clicking the segments; release the Shift button to create straight line segments. To undo a line segment, click the right and left mouse buttons simultaneously. Right-click to end the command.

F1>Lines>Semicircular creates a circular line. Left-click to activate and continue the semicircular line segments. For curved line segments, hold the Shift button down when left-clicking the segments; release the Shift button to create straight line segments. To undo a line segment, click the right and left mouse buttons simultaneously. Right-click to end the command. The curves of the semicircular lines are rounder than the curved lines created by the Bezier line.

F2>Tools>Rectangle creates a rectangular base piece. Click the desktop, drag the mouse, and click to place the piece.

F2>Orientation>X Sym moves the current sheet in relation to the x-axis. Click the pattern piece to activate the change.

F2>Orientation>Y Sym moves the current sheet in relation to the y-axis. Click the pattern piece to activate the change.

F3>Line modification>Len.Str.Line extends a line beyond the current pattern piece. Select an endpoint and drag the mouse to lengthen a line.

F3>Line modification>Merge changes an endpoint to a regular point. Select the point and click.

F3>Line modification>Simplify reduces the amount of variation in a curved line by reducing the tolerance in the line. Click the line, and select the amount of tolerance desired in the line.

F4>Piece>Cut creates a separate pattern piece from part of an existing pattern piece. Click inside the pattern piece. When the pattern piece turns green, right-click inside the same pattern piece. A new pattern piece is generated.

F5>Derived pieces>Cut Plot cuts a pattern piece apart along an internal line. Click an existing internal line to cut a pattern piece in two pieces. Two new pattern pieces are generated on two new sheets.

F5>Derived pieces>Sym2Pts to generate symmetry of a whole or part of a pattern piece. A new pattern piece is generated.

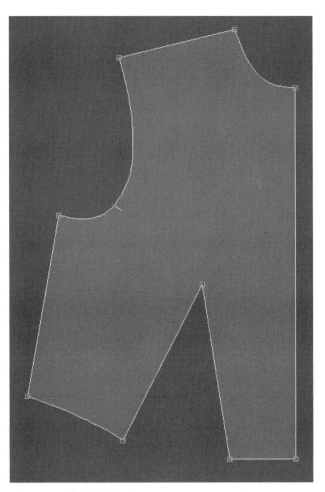

Figure 5.1 Right bodice front.

Creating a Left Front from a Right Front

When two sides of a garment are not symmetrical, the mirror image of a pattern will need to be created. If the two sides of a pattern piece are symmetrical, the second piece can be created in the variant.

Creating a Left Front from a Right Front

1. Digitize a bodice front or open the bodice file titled One-dart Bodice provided on the CD-ROM (Figure 5.1).

2. For a horizontally oriented pattern piece, select *F2>Orientation>X Sym* and click the pattern piece to create a left front.

3. For a vertically oriented pattern piece, select *F2>Orientation>Y Sym* and click the pattern piece to create a left front (Figure 5.2).

Turn-Back Facing or Attached Facing

Creating a Turn-Back Front Facing

1. Digitize a shirt front or open the bodice file titled One-dart Bodice provided on the CD-ROM (Figure 5.1).

2. To indicate the desired width of the facing, select *F1>Points>Add Point.* Add one point along the shoulder line and one point along the hemline to indicate the desired width of the facing.

3. To create the style line of the facing, select *F1>Lines>Bezier* to draw the front facing seam line. First, click outside the pattern piece beyond the hemline (outside the pattern piece). Then hold the Shift key down, click at the point where the facing starts to curve, click half the distance to the shoulder, and then right-click past the shoulder seam line (Figure 5.3). *F1>Lines>Semicircular* can also be used to create the facing style line. Hint: When the Shift key is held down, this creates curved lines; release the Shift key to create a straight line. A semicircular line creates a deeper arc than a Bezier line.

4. To create a full front, select *F5>Derived pieces>Sym2Pts,* click the dog-ear, and select *Mirror piece.* Then click the center front/hemline and the center front/ neckline intersection points. A new pattern piece is generated (Figure 5.4).

Figure 5.2 Left bodice front.

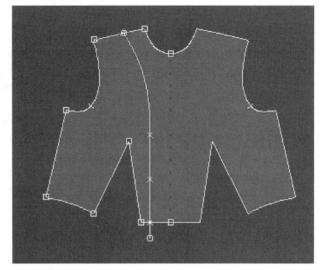

Figure 5.4 Full bodice front with Bezier line.

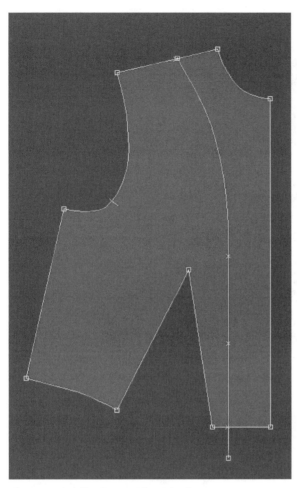

Figure 5.3 Bodice front with Bezier line.

5. To retain the front and facing as a single piece, select *F4>Piece>Cut* and click inside the desired piece with the left mouse button. The selected piece turns bright green when activated. Click inside the green area with the right mouse button. A new pattern piece is generated (Figure 5.5). Hint: All the required areas should be bright green.

Separate Front Facing

Creating a Separate Front Facing

1. Digitize a bodice front or open the bodice front file named One-dart Bodice provided on the CD-ROM (Figure 5.1).

2. To retain the original pattern piece, select *Sheet>Copy*.

3. Select *F1>Points>Add Point* and add points to the shoulder and hemlines at the desired width of the facing.

4. To create the facing style line, select *F1>Line>Bezier* to draw the front facing, and click outside the pattern piece beyond the hemline. Then hold the Shift key down, click at the point the facing starts to curve, click half the distance to the shoulder, and then right-click past the shoulder seam line to end the command (Figure 5.6). *F1>Line>Semicircular* can also be used to create the facing style line.

5. To retain only the front facing, select *F4>Piece>Cut* and click inside the facing with the left mouse. The piece turns bright green. Click inside green area with the right mouse button. A new pattern piece is generated (Figure 5.7).

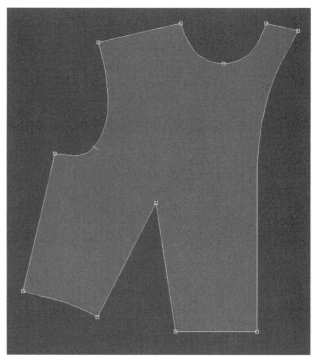

Figure 5.5 Bodice front with turn-back facing.

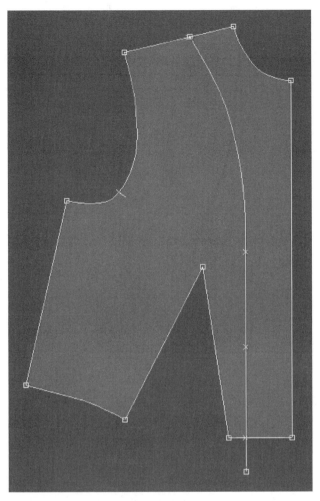

Figure 5.6 Bodice front with Bezier line.

Figure 5.7 Separate front facing.

Back Neck Facing

Creating a Back Neck Facing

1. Digitize a bodice back or open the bodice back file named One-dart Bodice provided on the CD-ROM. (Figure 5.1).

2. To create a full back, select *F5>Derived pieces>Sym2Pts,* and click the center back/hemline and the center back/neckline intersection points. A new pattern piece is generated.

3. To merge the neckline into one line, select *F3>Line modification>Merge* and click the center back/neckline point. The point is now changed to a regular point rather than an endpoint (Figure 5.8). Hint: If the line will not merge, select *F4>Industrialisation>Cut* and merge the neckline on the new pattern piece.

4. To create the back neck facing, select *F1>Lines>Parallel,* click the back neckline, and drag the mouse the desired width of the back neck facing. Left-click to place the parallel line. The width of the facing is indicated in the text box, or type "2″" in the textbox (Figure 5.9).

5. To create a back neck facing for an unlined garment, select *F4>Piece>Cut* and left-click inside the back neck facing. The pattern piece turns bright green. Then right-click inside the pattern piece.

6. To extend the end lines of the parallel line, set the **Curve prolongation** to 1″ in the dialog box (Figure 5.10). A new pattern piece is generated (Figure 5.11).

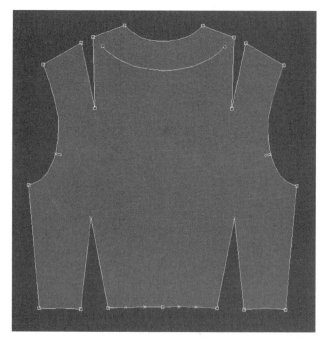

Figure 5.8 Full bodice back with merged neckline and parallel facing line.

Figure 5.9 Parallel text box.

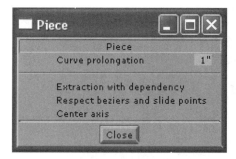

Figure 5.10 Curve prolongation dialog box.

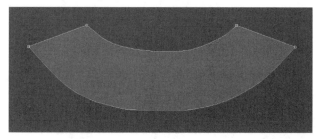

Figure 5.11 Back neck facing.

7. To trim the outer edge of the facing at the shoulder, add a point ⁵/₃₂″ down from the shoulder/facing outer edge intersection along the outer facing edge seam.

8. Attach the shoulder/facing outer edge endpoint to the new point to shorten the outer length of the facing at the shoulder. Hint: When the design has a lining, select *F5>Derived pieces>Cut Plot* to retain both pattern pieces. Two new pattern pieces are generated.

Sleeveless Bodice and Armhole Facing

The following steps include contouring and raising the side seam to create a fitted facing for a sleeveless bodice.

Creating Front Armscye Fitted Facing

Bodice Armhole Adjustments

1. Digitize a bodice front or open the bodice file named One-dart Bodice provided on the CD-ROM (Figure 5.1).

2. To raise the side seam up ¼″, select *F3>Line modification>Len.Str.Line.* Then add a point ¼″ up the extended line. The side seam can also be changed using *F3>Line modification>Reshape* to raise the armhole.

3. Using *F3>Point modification>Attach,* attach the original armscye/underarm point to the raised underarm point and reshape the armscye.

4. Using *F1>Points>Add Point,* add a point ½″ from the armscye/side seam intersection along the armscye.

5. Attach the armscye/underarm point to the point added in Step 4 and reshape the armscye. Hint: Curved points may need to be deleted along the armscye between the original underarm and the new point.

Separating the Facing

1. Select *F1>Lines>Parallel.* Click the armhole seam and drag the mouse the desired width of 1½" to 2". Then left-click to place the parallel line (Figure 5.12).

2. To create an armscye facing for an unlined garment, select *F4>Piece>Cut,* click the dog-ear, and change curve prolongation in the textbox to 1". This extends the cut 1" to the intersecting shoulder seam line. To cut the facing, left-click inside the facing area, and when the pattern piece turns bright green, right-click. Hint: If the entire pattern piece does not turn green, recheck the new facing line. A new pattern piece is generated (Figure 5.13).

3. To trim the outer edge of the facing at the shoulder, add a point ⁵⁄₃₂" down from the shoulder/facing outer edge intersection along the outer facing edge seam.

4. Using *F3>Point modification>Attach,* attach the shoulder/facing outer edge endpoint to the new point to shorten the outer length of the facing at the shoulder.

5. To trim the outer edge of the facing at the underarm, add a point ⁴⁄₃₂" from the side seam/facing outer edge intersection along the outer facing edge seam.

6. Attach the side seam/facing outer edge endpoint to the new point to shorten the outer length of the facing at the underarm. Hint: Delete any curve points between the endpoints and the new endpoints before attaching. When the design has a lining, select *F5>Derived pieces>Cut Plot* to retain both pattern pieces. Two new pattern pieces are generated.

Figure 5.12 Bodice front with armhole facing parallel line.

Figure 5.13 Armhole front fitted facing.

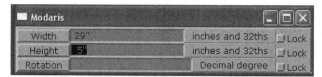

Figure 5.14 Rectangle text box.

Figure 5.15 Waistband draft.

Figure 5.16 Waistband.

Drafting

Drafting is a mechanical method of pattern development that uses measurements to create a pattern without the aid of blocks or slopers. Pattern pieces are created on the desktop rather than digitizing them into the computer. Any pattern piece can be created on the desktop. Common pieces created on the desktop include waistbands, collars, cuffs, pockets, and circular skirts.

Waistband

Creating a Waistband

1. Create a new sheet; select *Sheet>New Sheet*.

2. To draft a waistband, select *F2>Tools>Rectangle* and click the new sheet. Then type the width on-screen or the length of the waistband plus the extension (i.e., 29″) and the height on-screen or twice the width of the waistband (i.e., 5″) in the text box (Figure 5.14). You can drag the mouse to create a rectangle, but for long pattern pieces, the screen may not be large enough. Note: The width on-screen is the circumference of the waist plus any overlap. Hint: It is easier to type the amount needed in the text box for large or long pieces rather than trying to use the cursor to obtain the correct size (Figure 5.15).

3. Select *F4>Piece>Cut* and click inside the pattern piece. When the pattern piece turns bright green, right-click inside the pattern piece. A new pattern piece is generated (Figure 5.16).

4. Measure 1½″ in from the left end for the extension. Select *F1>Points>Add Point* or *F1>Lines>Parallel* to indicate the extension.

5. To place the notches at the waistband center front, select *F1>Points>Division* and divide the length of the waistband in half to indicate center front. Then select **F2>Notches>Notch** and replace the point with a notch. Repeat for side seam notches. Hint: Parallel lines can be used to line up notches, buttons, and buttonholes.

Cuffs

Creating a Cuff

1. Create a new sheet; select *Sheet>New Sheet.*

2. To create a rectangle on a new sheet, select *F2>Tools>Rectangle* and then drag the mouse the width or the circumference of the sleeve opening plus an extension or overlap for a button closure ($14\,^{16}/_{32}''\times 5''$; Figure 5.17). Then drag the mouse the height on-screen or twice the width of the cuff, or type the amount in the text box.

3. Select *F4>Piece>Cut* and click inside the pattern piece. When the pattern piece turns bright green, right-click inside the pattern piece. A new pattern piece is generated.

4. To place the notches for the cuff under-lap, first place a point, using *F1>Point> Developed,* to obtain the 1″ needed. Then select *F2>Notches>Notch* and replace the point with the notch. Repeat for the second notch.

5. To assist in button placement, you can use *F1>Lines>Parallel* to indicate the fold line.

6. Points are used to mark the button and buttonholes; select *F1>Points>Relative* (Figure 5.18). Hint: Parallel lines can be used to line up the button and buttonhole placement.

Figure 5.17 Cuff draft.

Figure 5.18 Cuff.

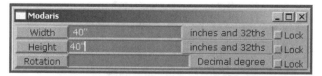

Figure 5.19 Rectangle text box.

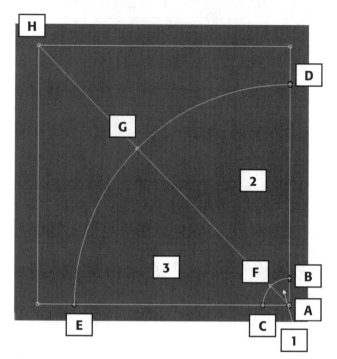

Figure 5.20 Circle skirt draft.

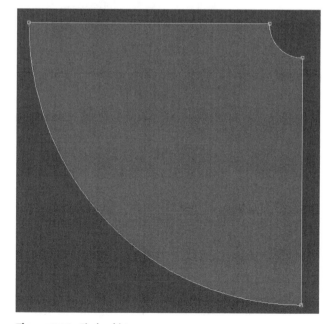

Figure 5.21 Circle skirt.

Circle Skirt

A circle skirt is created with a full circle at the hemline. Circle and half-circle skirts are created from the body waist measurement and the skirt length. The diameter of the waist measurement is used for half-circle skirts, and the radius measurement is used for circle skirts. For the diameter of the waist seam line for a half-circle skirt, the waist measurement is divided by $3\,{}^{1}/_{7}$. For the radius, the waist diameter is divided by 2.

Creating a Circle Skirt

1. Create a new sheet by selecting *Sheet>New Sheet.*

2. Draw a square the finished length of the skirt plus 10″. For example, create a square 40″ × 40″ for a skirt 30″ in length. Type the amount in the text box (Figure 5.19).

3. A to B is the waist radius, or 26″ ÷ 3 $^{1}/_{7}$″ = 8 $^{8}/_{32}$″ diameter (half-circle skirt). The waist diameter is then 8 $^{8}/_{32}$″ ÷ 2 = 4 $^{4}/_{32}$″ waist radius (full-circle skirt). (For calculations, see MacDonald, 2002.) See Figure 5.20. AB equals AC. Select *F1>Points> Developed* to place points at B and C.

4. Using *F1>Lines>Straight,* draw a straight line from A to H.

5. B to D is equal to the length of the skirt; BD equals CE. Select *F1>Points>Developed* to place points at D and E.

6. Select *F1>Lines>Semicircular* to create the waistline and the hemline. Hold the Shift key down to create a curved line. Click points B, F, and C for the waistline and points D, G, and E for the hemline.

7. Select *F4>Piece>Cut* and click areas 2 and 3. Both areas should be bright green. Then right-click to generate a new pattern piece (Figure 5.21). Hint: If areas 1 and 2 are selected, a **godet** is created.

Collars

Collars are designed to frame the face. The basic collar types include flat, full roll, convertible, partial role, and stand up.

Mandarin Collar

Stand-up collars such as a **mandarin collar** or collar band can be created with the following technique.

Creating a Mandarin Collar

1. Select Sheet>New Sheet.

2. Select F1>Line>Rectangle and draw a rectangle with a 1 1/2″ vertical line for the center back stand and the length of the neckline from center back to center front.

3. Using F1>Points>Add Point, add a point, to indicate the shoulder seam (Figure 5.22).

4. Using F1>Points>Add Point, add a point 1/2″ up from the neckline/center front intersection to give shape to the neckline edge of the collar.

5. Connect the points added in Steps 3 and 4 using F1>Lines>Bezier to create a curved collar neckline.

6. To develop the collar style line, select F1>Lines>Parallel. Click the Bezier line (neckline edge) from Step 4, and drag the mouse 1 1/2″ or the desired width of the collar. Right-click to place the line.

7. Connect the endpoints of the Bezier lines with F1>Lines>Straight.

8. To develop the pattern piece, use *F4>Piece>Cut* and click inside the two areas needed for the mandarin collar. A new pattern piece is derived (Figure 5.23).

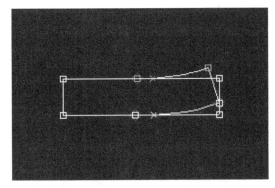

Figure 5.22 Mandarin collar draft.

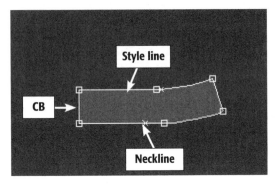

Figure 5.23 Mandarin collar.

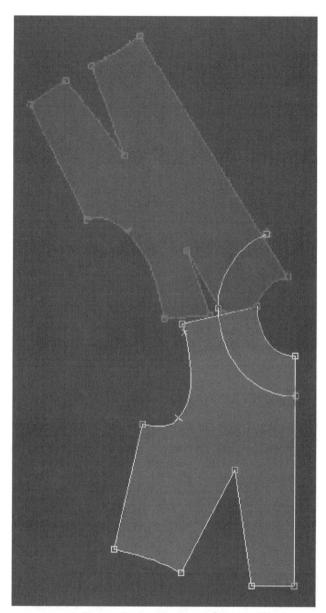

Figure 5.24 Bodice front and married back with Peter Pan parallel line.

Peter Pan Collar

The following method can be applied to **Peter Pan**, **sailor**, and **bertha collars**. The band of a shirt collar can also be developed with the following technique. Peter Pan collars can have a full roll, a partial roll, or a flat roll. The amount of overlap at the shoulder/armscye depends on the stand desired. A full-roll collar has a 4″ overlap, a partial-roll collar a 2″ overlap, and a flat-roll collar ½″.

Creating a Flat Peter Pan Collar

1. Digitize a bodice front or open the bodice front file named One-dart Bodice provided on the CD-ROM (Figure 5.1).

2. Select *F1>Point>Add Point* and add a point ½″ from the armscye/shoulder intersection on the armscye on the bodice front.

3. Select *F3>Line modification>Reshape* to raise the center back neck __″ for the collar neckline. Hint: Activate Print from the status bar menu located at the bottom of the screen to indicate the old and new collar necklines.

4. Select *F1>Line modification>Reshape* to lower the center front neckline ½″ down for the collar neckline and reshape the style line of the collar.

5. Select **F8>Assembly>Marry**. Marry the front and back bodices at the shoulder/neckline intersection point, click the center front/neckline intersection point of the bodice front, and move the cursor to the back/neckline intersection point of the bodice back. The two pieces are now temporarily attached together as a guide to create the Peter Pan collar (Figure 5.24).

6. Select **F8>Assembly>Pivot** and pivot the bodice front/back until there is a ½″ overlap at the shoulder/armscye.

7. To draw a line parallel with the front collar neckline, select *F1>Line>Parallel* and drag to the desired width of the collar or type the amount in the text box (Figure 5.25). Repeat for the back collar neckline. Join the front and back style lines of the collar at the shoulder with *F3>Point modification>Attach.*

8. Select *F4>Piece>Cut* to create the front and back collar areas. A new pattern piece is generated (Figure 5.26).

9. To curve the collar style line, add a point to the collar center front half the distance between the neckline and style line, and merge the endpoint of the center front/style line. Select *F3>Line modification> Reshape* to create the collar curve.

Shawl Collar

The **shawl collar** is designed with the collar and the bodice front cut as one. When the collar front rolls back, the lapel is created.

Creating a Shawl Collar

1. Digitize a bodice front or open the bodice front file named One-dart Bodice provided on the CD-ROM (Figure 5.1).

2. Select *F1>Line>Bezier* to add an extension beyond center front. Starting at the center front/waistline intersection, draw a line out 1″, then up to the bust level (breakpoint) to the shoulder/neckline intersection, and extend the line back neck length (Figure 5.27). Maintain a right angle at the shoulder seam.

3. Using *F1>Line>Parallel,* draw a line 2½″ for the width of the collar from the breakpoint to the center back. The line may be in two segments. If so, attach the points along the line, merge, and delete the point to create a straight style line.

Figure 5.25 Parallel line text box.

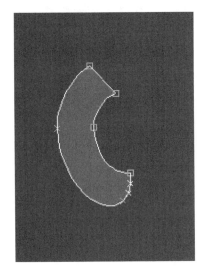

Figure 5.26 Peter Pan collar.

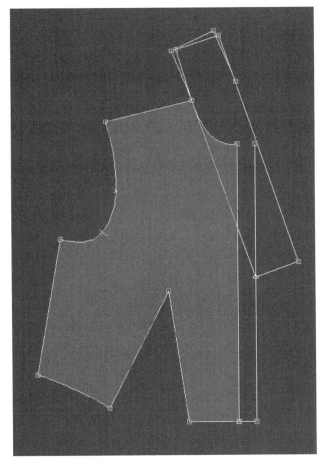

Figure 5.27 Bodice front with shawl collar draft.

Figure 5.28 Bodice front with shawl collar.

4. To extract the piece, use *F4>Piece>Cut* and select the original bodice, the collar pieces, and the center front overlap with the left mouse button. After all the pieces are selected for the new pattern, right-click to end the command (Figure 5.28).

5. Extend the center back seam of the collar ¼″ to the left using *F3>Line modification> Len.Str.Line.*

6. Using *F1>Line>Bezier,* draw a curved line from the shoulder point to the center back point created in Step 5.

7. Add a line parallel to the neckline (Bezier line) that reshapes the style line. Connect the two endpoints of the Bezier lines to create a new center back using a straight line.

8. To create the new shawl collar shape, use *F4>Piece>Cut* and select the bodice and collar areas, making sure to select the curve back neckline and style line. The breakline will be lost. Redraw the breakline from the breakpoint to the shoulder/neckline intersection. The original center front will also be lost; to replace the center front line, select *F1>Line>Parallel* and drag the mouse to the original center front line. Extend the center front 1″ by attaching it to the neckline, using *F3/ Point modification/Attach.*

9. To add the contour dart along the neckline, divide the neckline from the shoulder to the original center front in half. Place relative points ¼″ to the right and left of the division point. Use *F1>Line>Bezier* to connect the points for the contour dart (Figure 5.29).

Figure 5.29 Bodice front with shawl collar and fitting dart.

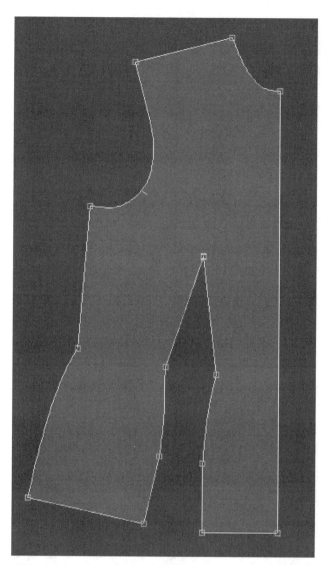

Figure 5.30 Jacket front.

Notched Collar

The **notched collar** is designed with a notch level with the base of the front neck or level with the jewel neckline. The shape of the lapel and the level of the notch can be varied to create a new design look.

Creating a Notched Collar

1. Digitize a jacket front or digitize the file named Jacket Front provided on the CD-ROM (Figure 5.30).

2. Extend the shoulder/neckline intersection 1″ using *F3>Line modification>Len.Str.Line* (Figure 5.31a).

3. Use *F1>Points>Add Point* to indicate the bust level (where the lapels overlap).

4. Move the center front out 1″ using *F1>Lines>Parallel* to create the extension.

5. Using *F1>Lines>Straight,* connect the endpoint through the point in Step 3, ending at the extension line.

6. The neck curve shape is needed as a guide for the lapel. To extract the neckline curve, select *F4>Piece>Cut* and click inside the neck or the **roll line** area of the collar.

7. *Marry* is a command most often used to check the accuracy of pattern pieces. It can also be used to line up two pattern pieces. Select *F8>Assembly>Marry* to marry the new piece by lining up the piece at the extended neckline/shoulder intersection. Using *F8>Assembly>Pivot,* line up the piece along the roll line.

8. Extend the line 1³/₄″ for the lapel collar upper edge with *F1>Lines>Straight.*

9. To draw a line perpendicular to center front starting at point E and extending 2″ toward the armhole, select *F1>Line> Straight.* Hint: If you are having difficulty creating a straight line that is perpendicular to center front, select *F1>Line> Parallel.* Click the hemline and drag the line up until it intersects with point E to serve as a guideline for the lapel line.

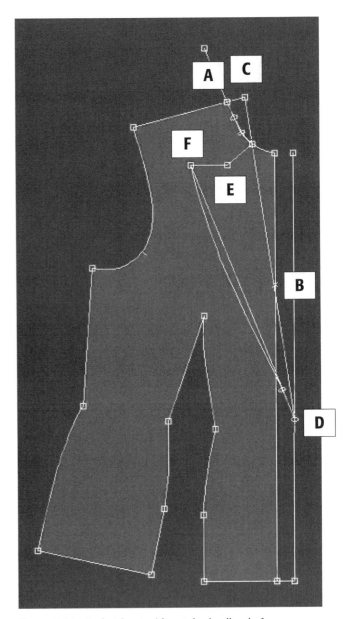

Figure 5.31a Jacket front with notched collar draft.

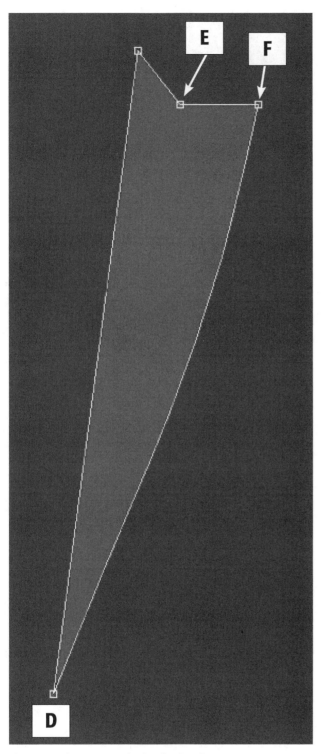

Figure 5.31b Front notched collar lapel.

10. Draw a straight line from the lapel line endpoint to breakpoint as a guideline. Shape the lapel, curving slightly outward using *F1>Lines>Bezier*. Hint: Zoom in to create a smoother style line by clicking on points and dragging them to a new position. Click to place them in the new position.

11. Cut the lapel out using *F4>Piece>Cut* by selecting all the pieces needed for the front collar lapel (Figure 5.31b).

12. The lapel needs to be symmetrical over the y-axis in order to create a mirror image that can then be attached to the roll line of the jacket at the breakpoint and the roll line/neckline intersection. Use *F2>Orientation>ysym* and attach to the roll line. At this time you may need to reshape the collar style line.

13. Add a point 1/4″ along the shoulder line toward the armhole.

14. Extend the neckline beyond the shoulder line back neck measurement + __" (Figure 5.32).

15. Using *F1>Points>Division,* divide the extended neckline in half and click the two endpoints. When the text box appears, type "2" and divide the neckline in half.

16. Square a line ½" away from the neckline.

17. The center back must be at a right angle to the collar neckline. To develop a right angle guide for the center back collar, create a rectangle on a new sheet. Then marry the rectangle at the neckline/center back collar intersection. Pivot the rectangle in place.

18. Using *F1>Lines>Straight,* draw the collar center back to the desired width of the collar.

19. Draw a straight line out from the shoulder/neckline intersection as a guide for the width of the collar equal to the center back width in Step 18.

20. Draw the style line of the collar from the center back through the guideline end-point developed in Step 17 and ending at the lapel upper edge. The style line should be parallel to the neckline from the center back/style line intersection to the point in Step 18. Smoothly curve toward the collar lapel, stopping ¾" from the lapel upper edge. Connect this endpoint with E in the lapel.

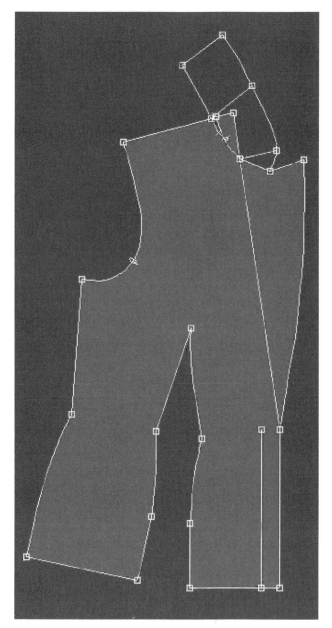

Figure 5.32 Jacket front with lapel and back notched collar draft.

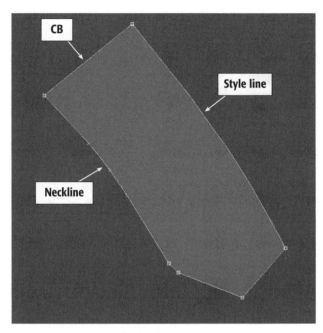

Figure 5.33 Back notched collar.

21. Use *F4>Piece>Cut* to select the three pattern pieces needed for the collar back with the left mouse button. After the pieces have been selected, end the command by selecting the right mouse button. A new pattern piece is derived (Figure 5.33).

Importing a Model

Importing one model into another can save time in the pattern-making process. Models or files can also be compared to one another. If pieces are missing from a model, one model can be imported into another model. Importing can also be used when a piece has been deleted and cannot be retrieved from the open model.

Importing a Model

1. Open a file or select the file named Bodice Model provided on the CD-ROM (Figure 5.34).

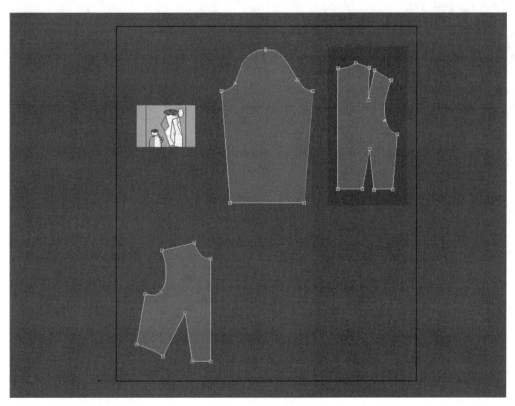

Figure 5.34 Bodice model.

2. Select *File>Import Model.* A text box appears (Figure 5.35).

3. Select the directory where the required pattern is located. For this exercise, select the One-dart Skirt file pattern found on the CD-ROM. This imports the skirt file into the bodice.

4. Select the right horizontal arrow. This places the file in the right-hand box.

5. Load the file. Multiple pattern pieces or files can be loaded into one file.

6. Close the text box. The new pattern pieces are now part of the file (Figure 5.36).

7. *Save* the file or *Save As* under a new name, as needed.

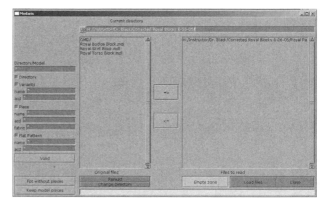

Figure 5.35 Import model text box.

Figure 5.36 Bodice and skirt model.

Exercises

1. Open a file or select the file named Chapter 5 Jacket provided on the CD-ROM. Create neck and armhole facings for the pattern pieces in the file.

2. Draft two patch pockets for the pattern front as indicated by the drill holes on the pattern front in the Chapter 5 Jacket file.

3. Open a file or select the file named Chapter 5 Bodice provided on the CD-ROM. Add a variation of a flat collar, such as a sailor or bertha collar, to the bodice.

4. Copy the basic jacket pattern and add a variation of a shawl collar to the jacket from Steps 1 and 2.

5. Copy the basic jacket pattern and add a variation of a notched collar to the jacket from Steps 1 and 2.

6. Import the Pant file provided on the CD-ROM located under Chapter 5 into the Jacket file from Steps 1 and 2.

Key Terms and Commands

F8>Assembly>Marry

F8>Assembly>Pivot

Bertha collar

Curve Prolongation

Godet

F3>Line modification>Len.Str.Line

F1>Lines>Parallel

Mandarin collar

Notched collar

F2>Notches>Notch

F2>Orientation>X Sym

F2>Orientation>Y Sym

Peter Pan collar

Roll line

Sailor collar

Shawl collar

F2>Tools>Rectangle

Completing a Pattern

6

A complete pattern has seam allowances, notches, drill holes, internal lines, and pattern identification information. Also presented in this chapter are commands for checking a pattern.

In this chapter, you will learn about the following:

- Completing a Pattern
- Buttons and Buttonholes
- Marking Buttons and Buttonholes
- Internal Details
- Notches
- Add Notches
- Seam Allowances
- Measuring Pattern Pieces
- Checking Pattern Pieces
- Measurements
- Pattern Identification Information
- Key Terms and Commands

Completing a Pattern

F1>Points>Add Point adds a characteristic point or a curve point at a relative distance from a reference or point. Click on a point, and then move the cursor to a new position and click.

F1>Points>Division adds points automatically at equal intervals when the user clicks two points on a line. A text box appears after the second point has been selected. In the pink area of the text box, type in the division number required for the spaces between the buttons, and then press the Enter key. The *division number* is the number of line segments required between two points. The number of line segments is one more than the number of points to be added.

F2>Notches>Notch places a notch along a seam line. Select the style of notch by clicking on the dog-ear to bring up the dialog box, and then click the notch type desired.

F2>Notches>Orientation reorients a notch by pivoting the notch end.

F3>Point modification>Merge connects two endpoints to create one line segment from two line segments. Click the endpoint.

F3>Pins>Pin constrains points in a fixed position during pattern manipulation commands such as *Move* and *Stretch*.

F3>Pins>Remove Pin unpins all the points on a pattern piece. Click the *Remove Pin* button and the pins are removed automatically.

F4>Industrialisation>Line seam applies a seam allowance to a seam line. When a new pattern piece is derived, the new pattern piece will have seam allowance. Apply a value to one or several seam lines of a pattern to create seam allowances.

F4>Industrialisation>Piece seam applies a seam allowance to a pattern piece. When a new pattern piece is derived, the new pattern piece will not have seam allowances. Apply beginning and ending seam values to the seams of a pattern piece. This command is used when seam allowances vary in width.

F4>Industrialisation>Change corner is used to create a new corner or to modify an existing corner.

F4>Industrialisation>Exchange Data is used to exchange the seam stitching line with the construction line of a pattern piece. The seam allowances toggle on and off.

F5>Derived pieces>Cut2Pts cuts a pattern piece between two points of a pattern piece. Click two existing points to cut a pattern piece in two pieces. Two new pattern pieces are generated on two new sheets.

F8>Assembly>Marry temporarily attaches pattern pieces together for checking. The command is used to match two or more pattern pieces or seam allowances in order to check that pieces are the correct lengths.

F8>Assembly>Move marriages changes the attached position or points of married pattern pieces.

F8>Assembly>Pivot is used after two pieces are married to rotate the pieces to line pattern pieces or seam allowances. Hint: Hold the Shift key down to flip a pattern piece.

F8>Assembly>Walking Pcs. checks the accuracy of pattern pieces. Prior to walking, the pieces must be married. To assemble two pieces together, click the starting point that is attached on the two pieces. Start walking by sliding the cursor along the line to match. Button 3 of the computer mouse freezes the walking to enable reshaping of the pattern pieces.

F8>Assembly>Divorce separates married pieces. Click the piece to be separated. Hint: Divorced pieces can be found in the lower right-hand side of the desktop. Select J on the keyboard to rearrange all the pattern pieces.

Buttons and Buttonholes

Adding buttonholes to a garment is a two-step process. The first step is to create the center front overlap extension, and the second is to place the button and buttonholes.

Creating a Center Front Extension and Placing Button Closures

1. Digitize a bodice front or open the bodice front file named One-dart Bodice provided on the CD-ROM (Figure 6.1).

2. Add two points, one at the neckline and one at the hemline, each $1/2''$ from the center front seam line. Select *F1 Point> Developed.* The new points will be used to hold the pattern in place except for the center front seam line. Hint: Click the dog-ear to select the type of point desired. Remember that *No mark* is the default.

3. Select *F3>Pins>Pin* and click on the two new points. Pinning is automatically activated. Hint: Any points attached to a line can be pinned.

4. Activate *Print* on the status bar menu at the bottom of the screen before extending the center front to indicate the original center front line. The original center front line is needed for placement of the button and buttonholes.

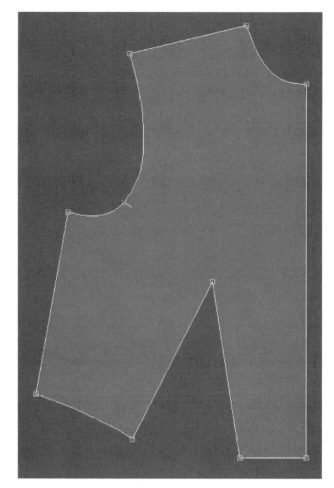

Figure 6.1 One-dart bodice front.

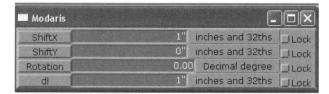

Figure 6.2 Move text box.

Figure 6.3 Bodice front with center front extension.

5. Extend the center front, select *F3>Line modification>Move,* and click the middle of the center front seam line. Then drag the mouse the required amount for an extension. Note: When a vertical extension is desired, in the text box, for a 1″ extension, *ShiftX* and *dl* should be at 1″, while *ShiftY* and *Rotation* remain constant at 0 (Figure 6.2). When a horizontal extension is desired, *ShiftY* and *dl* should be at 1″, while *ShiftX* and *Rotation* remain constant at 0. Hint: If your point is not remaining in place after it is pinned, display curve points and zoom in to make sure you are picking the correct point.

6. Select *F1>Line>Parallel* to place a line at the original center front line (Figure 6.3).

Marking Buttons and Buttonholes

Marking the Buttons

1. Create a front bodice with an extension. Activate *Sheet>Copy* and click the pattern piece created in the previous section, or open the Bodice front with extension file provided on the CD-ROM (Figure 6.3).

2. To determine the placement of the top and bottom buttons, select *F1>Points>Relative point* and place the top and bottom buttons along the original center front. Note: Click the dog-ear to select the type of point desired. Hint: *No mark* is the default but will not leave a point when a new pattern piece is generated (Figure 6.4).

Figure 6.4 Bodice front extension with top and bottom buttons.

Figure 6.5 Bodice front extension with buttons.

Figure 6.6 Division text box.

3. To place the remaining buttons between the top and bottom buttons (Figure 6.5), select *F1>Points>Division* and click the top and bottom buttons on the center front. The text box opens (Figure 6.6). In the pink area, type in the division number that is the number equal to the spaces between the buttons. Note: The division number is one higher than the number of buttons required.

Internal Details

Internal details include welt pocket lines and drill holes. You can add internal details when digitizing or during pattern work at the computer. Drill holes are used to indicate appliqué and pocket placement.

Creating Drill Holes for Pocket Placement

1. Digitize a torso front or open the Torso Front file provided on the CD-ROM.

2. Select *F1>Points>Relative point* and click for placement of one end of the pocket. Hint: The first relative point is measured from another point on the garment, such as the underarm/side seam intersection.

3. Select *F1>Points>Relative point* and click on the first drill hole. Then move the mouse to the length of the pocket to place the second drill hole as in the case of the upper pocket (Figure 6.7).

4. For a welt pocket, select *F1>Points> Relative point* to place the first end of the pocket, and then *F1>Lines>Straight* to create the welt line.

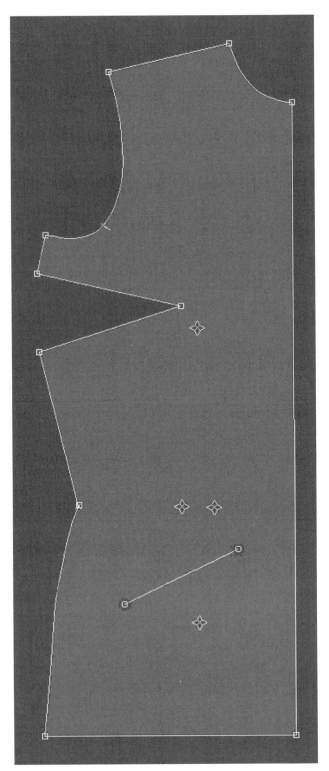

Figure 6.7 Torso front with pocket placement.

Figure 6.8a Text notches text box.

Figure 6.8b Icon notches text box.

Notches

Notches are important in pattern work for accuracy. Notches are placed perpendicular to a seam line. Modaris has four types of notches to choose from (Figures 6.8a and b).

Notching

1. Digitize a bodice front or open the bodice front file named One-dart Bodice provided on the CD-ROM (Figure 6.1).

2. Select *F2>Notches>Notch*. To select the type of notch, click the dog-ear and choose a notch type. The notch text box can be toggled from text to icon. Click the line at the point where the notch is to be placed.

3. To move a notch along a line, select *F3>Modification>Reshape*. The notch can be slid up or down the seam line it is attached to.

4. *F2>Notches>Orientation* moves a notch manually in a circle around the line to which it is attached.

5. *F2>Notches>Perpendicular* orients a notch 90 degrees to the line to which it is attached.

Seam Allowances

Modaris has two options for adding seam allowances: line seam and piece seam.

Adding Seam Allowances to a Pattern Piece

1. Digitize a bodice front or open the bodice front file named One-dart Bodice provided on the CD-ROM (Figure 6.1).

Option 1:

1. Select *F4>Industrialisation>Piece seam* to apply one seam allowance to the new seam lines. Click each line to add the seam allowance. A text box opens. Type in the seam allowance width—for example, $^{16}/_{32}''$ for a $^1/_2''$ seam allowance. Press the Enter key. The amount typed in the first pink area appears in the second pink area of the text box (Figure 6.9). Press Enter again if the seam allowance is to remain constant. Note: If the cursor is not in the pink area, the box will not close. The cursor can also be moved the desired width of the seam allowance from the original seam line. Click to place the seam line. If after you add seam allowances to a pattern, the piece does not indicate seam allowances, select *F4>Industrialisation> Exchange Data*. The seam allowances can now be viewed.

Figure 6.9 Seam allowance text box.

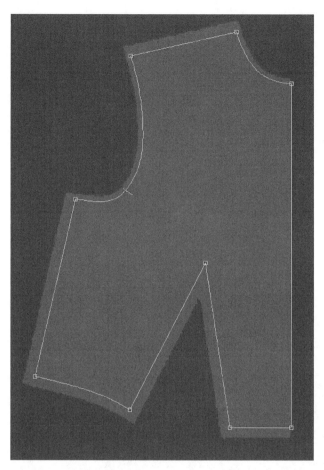

Figure 6.10 Bodice front with seam allowances.

Option 2:

1. Select *F4>Industrialisation>Line Seam* to add seam allowances by applying a beginning seam value and an end seam value. Hint: Hold the Shift key down to select all construction lines, and then apply the seam value at one time. You need to select the piece, either with the selection button or by right-clicking it. If after you add seam allowances to a pattern piece, the piece does not indicate seam allowances, select *F4>Industrialisation>Exchange Data*. The seam allowances can now be viewed.

Adding Seam Allowances to a New Style Line

1. Create a bodice front with seam allowances (Figure 6.10).

2. Add two points on each seam line to indicate the placement of the new style line by selecting *F1>Points>Add Point* and clicking on the lines.

3. Select *F1>Line>Straight* to add a seam line. Click the two points placed in Step 2.

4. To add seam allowances to the new seam line, select *F4>Industrialisation>Line seam*, and click the new style line. A text box appears (Figure 6.9). Add the desired width of the seam allowance. To validate the command, press the Enter key. Select *F4>Industrialisation>Exchange Data* to display the seam allowances.

5. To cut the new seam line, select
   F5>Derived pieces>Cut Plot and click the
   internal line. New pattern pieces are
   generated (Figure 6.11). Hint: If a seam
   allowance does not fill in accurately, select
   F4>Piece>Cut. This creates a new pattern
   piece without seam allowances. The seam
   allowances can then be reapplied and will
   fill in accurately. If after you add seam
   allowances to a pattern piece, the piece
   does not indicate seam allowances, select
   F4>Industrialisation>Exchange Data. The
   seam allowances can now be viewed.

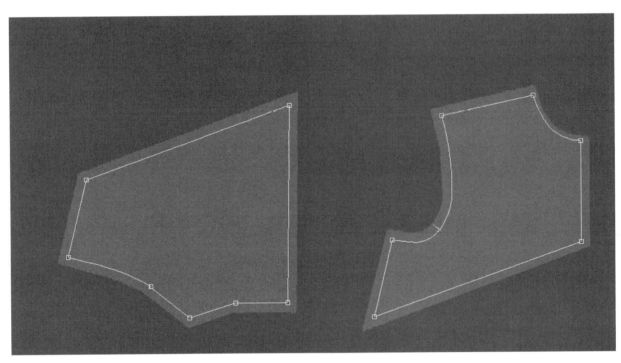

Figure 6.11 Bodice yoke and lower front with seam
allowances.

Figure 6.12a Icon seam allowance corner variations text box.

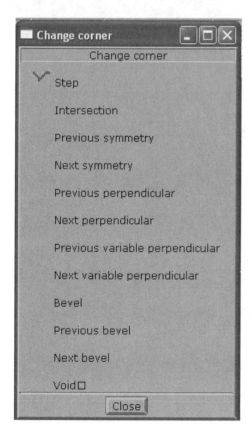

Figure 6.12b Text seam allowance corner variations text box.

Seam Allowances with Corner Variations

Once seam allowances have been added, the corners can be shaped. Accurate seam allowance corners assist sewers in lining up garment pieces when sewing. Corners can be angled to save fabric when markers are made.

Corner Tools

The type of corner selected is dependent on the type of pattern pieces being sewn together. The type of corners to select can be found under the drop-down menu corner tool, *F4>Industrialisation>Add corner*, or on the top line of the status bar menu, as indicated in Chapter 1. If a corner has previously been selected, then *F4>Industrialisation> Change corner* can also be used to select a corner. To select a specific corner, click the dog-ear to reveal the corner tools dialog box (Figure 6.12a and b).

Beveling Seam Allowance Corners

1. To change the seam allowance corners, select *Tools>Corner.*

2. Select the correct corner variation.

3. Click on the corner to apply the new corner. Hint: Corner tools will only work when the seam value is defined and displayed (Figures 6.13 and 6.14). If the corner is rounded in shape, change the corner point to an endpoint by selecting *F3>Point modification>Section.*

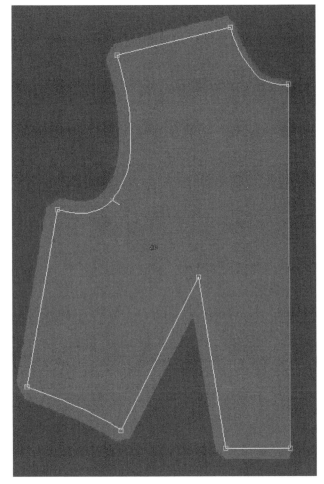

Figure 6.13 Bodice front with beveled corners.

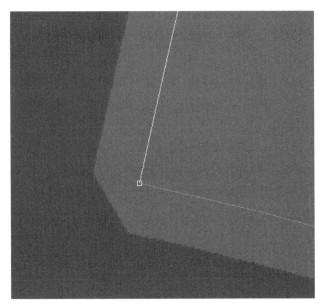

Figure 6.14 Close-up of a beveled corner.

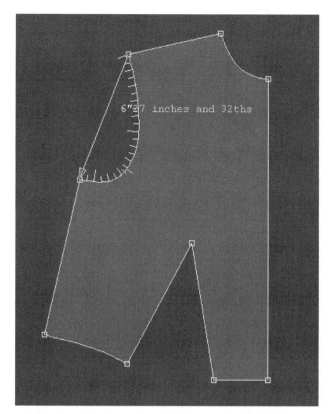

Figure 6.15 Bodice front with length measurement of the armhole.

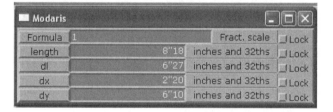

Figure 6.16 Length text box.

Measuring Pattern Pieces

Checking pattern pieces during pattern making is essential for maintaining accuracy. Modaris has a variety of measurement tools for checking patterns. Seam and seam length automatically display the distance measured. The seam and seam length distance is also placed in a spreadsheet.

Checking Patterns

1. Digitize a bodice front or open the bodice front named One-dart Bodice provided on the CD-ROM (Figure 6.1). To check the length of straight or curved lines of a pattern, select *F8>Measurements>Length* (Figure 6.15). A text box opens indicating the length of the seam; *Length* in the text box is the actual seam length (Figure 6.16). Click the endpoint of a seam line of a pattern piece. Then move the cursor to the opposite endpoint. *Length* can also be used to measure pattern pieces internally. Do not press the Enter key or the measurement will no longer be visible. The length distance is also automatically placed in the spreadsheet (Figure 6.17).

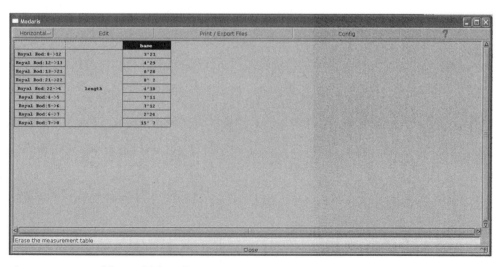

Figure 6.17 Spreadsheet with length measurement.

2. To check or view straight or curved seam lengths, select *F8>Measurements>Seam Length* (Figure 6.18). Click the endpoint of a seam line and move the cursor to the opposite endpoint and click. The seam length appears. Do not click the Enter key or the measurement will no longer be visible. The cut and seam length distance is also automatically placed in the spreadsheet (Figure 6.19).

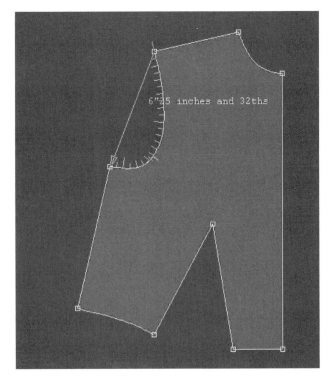

Figure 6.18 Bodice front with seam length measurement of the armhole.

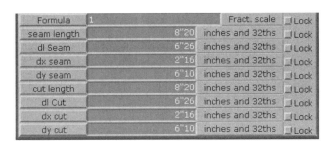

Formula	1		Fract. scale	Lock
seam length	8"20	inches and 32ths		Lock
dl Seam	6"26	inches and 32ths		Lock
dx seam	2"16	inches and 32ths		Lock
dy seam	6"10	inches and 32ths		Lock
cut length	8"20	inches and 32ths		Lock
dl Cut	6"26	inches and 32ths		Lock
dx cut	2"16	inches and 32ths		Lock
dy cut	6"10	inches and 32ths		Lock

Figure 6.19 Seam length text box.

Checking Pattern Pieces

Checking pattern pieces on the computer should follow the same procedure as checking patterns by hand. Checking should include matching all seams and notches that are going to be sewn together.

The spreadsheet shown in Figure 6.20 displays the measurements of one or several pattern pieces. *Length* measures the distance between two points in a straight line. To check the length of a seam, select *F8>Measurements>Seam Length,* which measures the distance between two points or notches along a seam, and then click the seam to be measured.

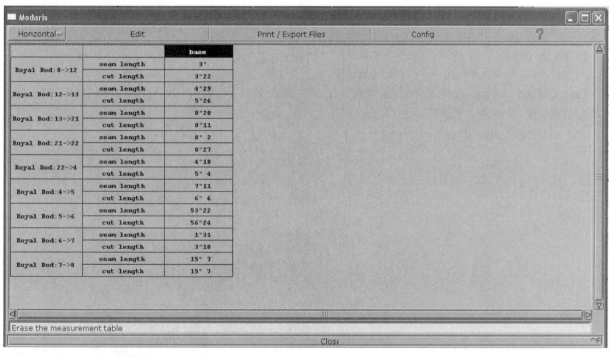

Figure 6.20 Spreadsheet with seam length and cut length measurements.

Checking Front and Back Pattern Pieces

1. Open the Pattern to Check file provided on the CD-ROM.

2. To check the front and back shoulder seams, select *F8>Assembly>Marry,* matching the front and back pattern pieces at the neckline/shoulder seam intersection points (Figure 6.21). Click the front underarm point and move the cursor over the back underarm point. Click to position the front piece over the back. Hint: Zoom to check that the front and back pieces are accurately matched.

3. Line up the side seams using *F8>Assembly>Pivot.* Click the side seam and rotate the front pattern piece until the side seams are aligned (Figure 6.22). Using *F8>Assembly>Move marriages,* check the length from the armhole. Place a notch to accurately check the shoulder seam length. Hint: Click along the side seam; the farther from the pivot point, the easier it is to control the rotation of the pattern piece.

Figure 6.21 Front and back bodice married at the center front and center back neckline.

Figure 6.22 Front and back bodice married and pivoted with shoulder seams matching.

Figure 6.23 Front and back bodice with matching front and back armhole.

4. If the side seams are not exactly the same length, select *F3>Point modification> Reshape* to modify seam lengths or shapes.

5. To check a second seam line, the pattern pieces must be repositioned. Select *F8>Assembly>Move marriages.* Click the front piece at the neckline/shoulder seam intersection point and match it to the back at the same location. Click to place the piece.

6. Select *F8>Assembly>Pivot* to rotate the front pattern piece until the shoulder seams are lined up. Check the shoulder seam lengths. The neckline shape can also be checked for a smooth curve from center front to center back. Note: Check for 90-degree corners at the neckline/ shoulder seam intersection point (Figure 6.23).

7. Separate married pattern pieces by selecting *F8>Assembly>Divorce* and clicking on the sheets. The pattern pieces automatically separate onto two separate sheets. Hint: J on the keyboard allows viewing of all the pieces.

Checking Front and Sleeve Pattern Pieces

1. To check a curved seam with two different shaped curves, such as an armhole and a sleeve, you need to rotate the pieces. Select *F8>Assembly>Marry,* matching the two pieces at the underarm/side seam intersection point.

2. Select *F8>Assembly>Walking Pcs.* Click the point on the piece to walk, and then click the point of the piece to remain stationary (Figure 6.24).

3. Hint: Use the Shift key if the walking piece needs to be flipped. Use the mouse to control the walking movement. The piece moves along the sew line. Left-click to stop the walking. Zoom to enlarge the curve. The blue pattern piece is the base piece, the green is the married piece, and the outline indicates the amount walked.

4. To smooth out seam lines, select *F3>Point modification>Reshape* as needed.

5. Continue walking by clicking on the common points of the two pieces with the left button.

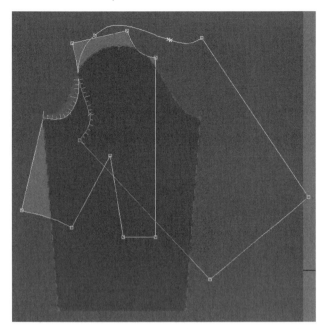

Figure 6.24 Bodice front and walking the sleeve.

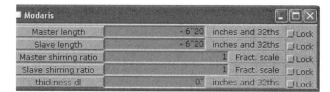

Figure 6.25 Walking pieces text box.

6. To stop walking to modify the pattern pieces, select *F8>Assembly>Walking Pcs.* When your pattern needs correction, click the left mouse button to stop walking or click on-screen at the desired point to freeze the pattern pieces. Click the right button to freeze walking, and the left button to continue walking. The walking pieces text box indicates the length of the bottom pattern piece or the master piece. The master piece length can be compared with the slave piece or the top pattern pieces. In the example, the side seam length can be compared (Figure 6.25). If the lengths are not the same, select *F3>Point modification>Reshape* as needed to smooth or lengthen seams. Left-click to continue checking the sleeve and right-click to exit walking.

7. To separate married pattern pieces, select *F8>Assembly>Divorce* and click the sheet. The pattern pieces automatically separate. Hint: J on the keyboard allows viewing of all the pieces.

Checking Skirt Front and Back

Side seams of a skirt are balanced when the angle of the front side seam is the same as the angle of the back side seam.

1. To check the side seams, select *F8>Assembly>Marry,* matching the front and back skirt pattern pieces at the waist/side seam intersection points (Figure 6.26).

2. The side seam should match, and the center front and center back seam allowances should be parallel. Use *F3>Point modification>Reshape* to correct the pattern pieces.

3. Select *F8>Assembly>Divorce* to separate the two pieces.

4. To check the shape of the hem, select *F2>Orientation>YSym.* This orients the selected sheet in the opposite direction.

Figure 6.26 Married skirt front and back.

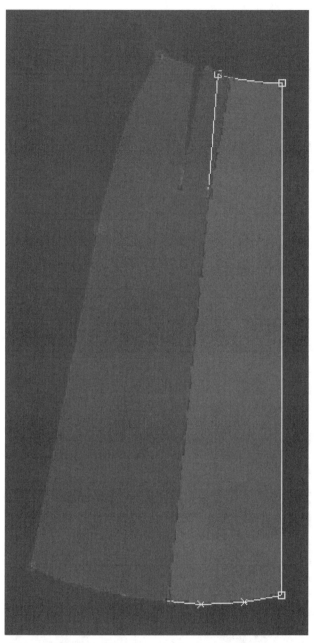

Figure 6.27 Married skirt front and back at the side seam.

5. To check the hem shape, select *F8>Assembly>Marry,* matching the front and back waist/side seam intersection points (Figure 6.27).

6. Select *F3>Point modification>Reshape* to smooth the shape of the hem.

7. Select *F8>Assembly>Divorce* to separate the front and back pattern pieces. To view all pattern pieces in the file, press J on the keyboard.

Pattern Identification Information

Labeling pattern work for identification is important. The pattern piece names and variant names are limited to nine characters maximum. The comment field is limited to 32 characters maximum.

Naming a Pattern Piece or a Field in a Title Block

1. Select *Display>Title Block.*

2. Select *Edit>Edit.*

3. Click the pattern piece (Figure 6.28 a) or inside the title block field (Figure 6.28 b).

4. Input the name inside the pattern piece. Remember that pattern names are limited to nine characters.

Figure 6.28a A bodice front.

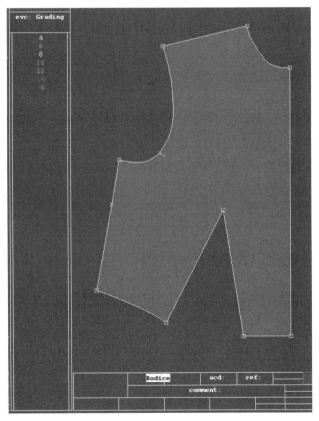

Figure 6.28b Bodice front with title block.

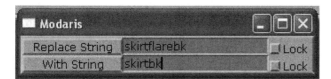

Figure 6.29 Text box for renaming a pattern piece.

Renaming a Pattern Piece or a Field in a Title Block

1. Right-click the sheet to be renamed. The pattern piece turns green.

2. Select *Edit>Rename.* The *Replace* text box appears (Figure 6.29).

3. Replace the old name, shown in the *Replace String* field, with the new name by typing it into the *With String* field. Press Enter to validate.

Adding Special Text

Special text can be added in the apparel industry for a variety of information, including *Hold for Fuse, Embroidery,* and *Appliqué.*

1. To add special text to a pattern piece, select *F4>Industrialisation>Axis,* click the dog-ear, and select *Special Axis* in the dialog box that appears. Click at the start point and then at the endpoint. Hint: Hold the Ctrl key down to rotate the text line in 45-degree increments.

2. Select *Edit>Edit* and click the axis. Type pattern information or name the pattern piece.

When naming consecutive pattern pieces, select the first pattern piece by using the current sheet or by right-clicking on the piece to activate. Select *Edit>Edit* and click the title bar labeled *Name.* Use the keyboard arrows to key in the piece abbreviation (see Appendix C for abbreviations). Continue to page down to repeat the process with each additional sheet.

Exercises

1. To practice adding notches to a pattern, open the file named Notches provided on the CD-ROM. Add notches or correct the notches on the pattern pieces.

2. To practice adding seam allowances, open the file named Seam Allowance provided on the CD-ROM. Add seam allowance and corners to the seam allowances.

3. To grade buttons, open the file named Torso with Buttons provided on the CD-ROM and grade the buttons.

4. Open the file named Pattern Pieces to Check II provided on the CD-ROM. Check the pattern pieces for accuracy using the commands described on pages 140–145.

5. To practice renaming the pattern pieces, open the file named Renaming provided on the CD-ROM.

Key Terms and Commands

F8>Assembly>Divorce

F8>Assembly>Marry

F8>Assembly>Move marriages

F8>Assembly>Pivot

F8>Assembly>Walking Pcs.

F5>Derived pieces>Cut2Pts

F4>Industrialisation>Change corner

F4>Industrialisation>Exchange Data

F4>Industrialisation>Line seam

F4>Industrialisation>Piece seam

F2>Notches>Notch

F2>Notches>Orientation

F3>Pins>Pin

F3>Pins>Remove Pin

F3>Point modification>merge

F1>Points>Add Point

F1>Points>Division

Pattern Grading

7

Grading is the process of proportionally increasing or decreasing a master pattern. Pattern grading using a computer is both accurate and efficient. This chapter outlines pattern grading on the computer. For information on pattern grading principles or calculating the amount of grading at a point, please refer to a pattern grading textbook, such as *Concepts of Pattern Grading* by Moore, Mullet, and Young (2001).

In this chapter, you will learn about the following:

- General Guidelines for Pattern Grading
- Commands for Pattern Grading
- Sizing a Pattern
- Grade Rules
- Grading a New Shape
- Transfer Grading
- Grading Buttonholes
- Control Grading
- Key Terms and Commands

General Guidelines for Pattern Grading

Computer pattern grading or pattern movement is based on the **Cartesian graph** concept (Moore, Mullet, and Young, 2001). The pattern piece orientation is the first decision that must be established. As shown in Figure 3.3, the point of reference is 0,0 (zero,zero), and the x- and y-coordinates of a **grade rule** for a point are based on the pattern orientation or the direction the pattern is positioned. Each **grade point** is found in one of four quadrants formed by the x- and y-axes. The procedure for calculating grade rules on the computer is the same as for calculations done manually. Understanding the Cartesian graph is the foundation for applying pattern grading rules.

The incremental changes for the basic pattern pieces in this chapter are 1″ grade between sizes 6–8 and 8–10, and 1½″ grade between 10–12, 12–14, and 14–16.

Commands for Pattern Grading

F6>Grading control>Control is used to input and modify grade values of specific points for sizes. Once the control button is selected, a text box opens and the grade values can be input. The user types in the **dx** and **dy** values, while the computer calculates the other values automatically.

F6>Grading control>Nest is used to display a nest or a set of pattern pieces, showing all the sizes in a size range stacked along a common reference line. The **graded nest** is displayed on-screen and shows the differences for each successive size.

F6>Grading control>Eff. Packing is used to save the shape with the desired nest pack.

F6>Grading modification>Free grading deletes the grade rules of selected points.

F6>Grading modification>ReportX reports the x movement from one grade point to a second grade point.

F6>Grading modification>ReportY reports the y movement from one grade point to a second grade point.

F6>Grading modification>Equate allows the transfer of grade points from one point to a second point. The points can be on the same or different pattern pieces. Click point 1 of the graded point, and then click point 1 of a nongraded point.

F6>Grading modification>Cancel. Grading cancels the previous grade, and a 0,0 grade for the x- and y-axis is reported. Click a previously graded point to change the grade rules to 0,0.

F6>Grading modification>GraPro assigns proportional grading at 2 points, as well as to all points located on the curve(s) between the two points. This blends the grading between two reference points. Click the two points, holding the mouse down on the second point.

F6>Grading modification>Pro 2Pts grades a point or points proportionally when the user right-clicks on all the points. Click on the first reference point, and then click on the two reference points. The points take on proportional grading.

F6>Grading modification>XSym is used to flip a grade point from top to bottom, or in a horizontal pivot direction. Select the *XSym,* and then click the point to pivot.

F6>Grading modification>YSym is used to flip a grade point from right to left, or in a vertical pivot direction. Select the *YSym,* and then click the point to pivot.

F6>Grading modification>RepSq is used to transfer grade rules, or a series points is transferred from one pattern piece to a second pattern piece. Click the first point of a graded pattern piece, hold down the space-bar, and click the last point in a series of the graded pattern piece. Then click point 1 of the nongraded pattern piece and the last point in a series of the nongraded pattern piece.

F7> Evolution System>Imp.EVT is used to import a size range for a new style. Click the model sheet (the sheet with the yellow little bar around it) to bring up the file directory.

F7> Evolution System>Rep.EVT is used to add sizing to all sheets in a file. Choose *Selection>Select all Sheets,* and click all the sheets that require sizing in the file. Then select *F7>Evolution System>Rep.EVT* and choose the sizing required.

Sizing a Pattern

Sizing or creating a graded nest can be done prior to digitizing or after digitizing. Before pattern grading, select *Display>Title Block*. As indicated in Chapter 3, a text file is used to create a size table. If no size table has been generated, *F10* will generate a generic table for pattern pieces. When the title block is engaged, a yellow box is displayed around the sheets in a model. *Select F7>Evolution System>IMP.EVT* to import a size range for a new style. Click the model sheet to bring up the file directory.

Grade Rules

The grading of a point is done by modifying or inputting new grade values, referred to as grade rules. The grade rules for grade points are displayed in a control table (Figure 7. 1). The values correspond to the *x* and *y* in relation to the basic or base size and are represented by *dx* and *dy* in the control table. *DL* represents the distance between a size and the base size on a straight line. *Ddx* and *ddy* represent the linear distance between two sizes, and *ddl* represents the linear length between two sizes. *Dx* and *dy* are input by the user, whereas *dl, ddx, ddy,* and *ddl* are values automatically calculated by the computer (Figure 7.2).

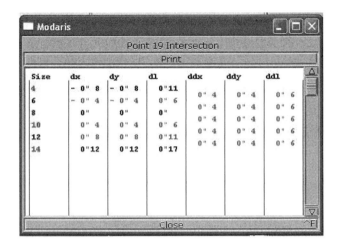

Figure 7.1 Control window.

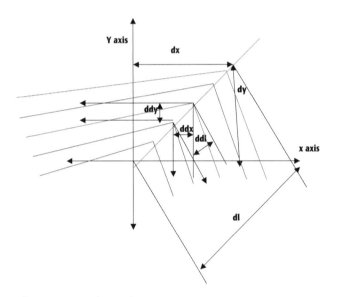

Figure 7.2 X and y grade movements.

Depending on the control point type, some parameters cannot be modified. The parameters for a slider or developed point on the *dl* and the *ddl* can be modified, and the parameters for a characteristic or relative point on the *dl* cannot be modified. None of the parameters for a linked point can be modified. As shown in Figure 7.1, the break sizes are displayed in red and the base size is indicated in blue.

The amount that grade rules change from one size to the next is called the incremental value. In this chapter, the grading incremental values are calculations based on 32nds of an inch. This means that $1\frac{1}{2}''$ is $^{32}/_{32}$ (1″) + $^{16}/_{32}''$ ($\frac{1}{2}''$); therefore, 48 would be the number entered. The numerator, or top number, of a fraction is the number entered in the control table. Grading can be viewed on the desktop by selecting function keys (Table 7.1).

Table 7.1 Pattern Grading Function Key Commands

Function Key	Command
F9	Graded nest display
F10	Displays only the base size, no grading
F11	Displays the break sizes of grading
F12	Displays all sizes of grading

Grading a New Shape

1. Digitize a one-dart bodice or open the one-dart bodice file named Grading Bodice provided on the CD-ROM.

2. Select the bodice front, and right-click the sheet. Always check to make sure the pattern piece is in the correct position for the grade rules.

3. Select *Display>Display Title Block.*

4. Select *F6>Grading Control>Control,* and then click the grade point of a pattern piece to open the control window. The control window can remain open while grading an entire piece or pieces. Arrow up or down takes the cursor one size up or down in the control window.

5. Refer to Figure 7.3 and Table 7.2 for grading the bodice front, sizes 4 to 14.

6. Click point 2 on the bodice front sheet located on the desktop. In the case of the bodice front, point 2 is the starting point, since point 1 does not have any incremental changes.

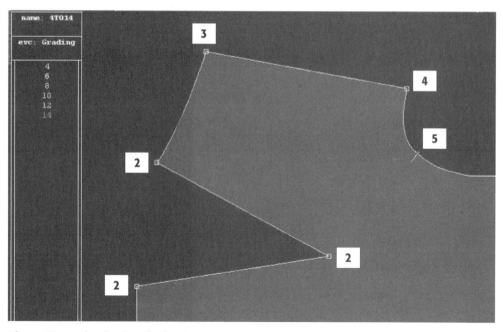

Figure 7.3 Grade rules for a bodice front.

Table 7.2 Grade for a Basic Bodice Front

Size	Rule 1 DX DY	Rule 2 DX DY	Rule 3 DX DY	Rule 4 DX DY	Rule 5 DX DY	Rule 6 DX DY	Rule 7 DX DY	Rule 8 DX DY
4	0 0	0 −8	0 −24	−8 −24	0 0	−16 −10	−18 −4	−16 0
6	0 0	0 −4	0 −12	−4 −12	0 0	−8 −6	−10 −2	−8 0
8	0 0	0 0	0 0	0 0	0 0	0 0	0 0	0 0
10	0 0	0 4	0 12	4 12	0 0	8 6	20 4	8 0
12	0 0	0 8	0 24	8 24	0 0	8 12	30 8	16 0
14	0 0	0 12	0 36	12 36	0 0	12 24	40 12	24 0

Figure 7.4 Graded nest for a bodice front.

7. Click on size 4 dx space in the control chart, and type in the grade amount. Enter the dx and dy grade amounts in the control chart for point 2. These amounts represent the grade change from size 8, or the base size.

8. Click point 3 of the bodice front pattern piece, and then enter the dx and dy values for all sizes.

9. Continue to enter each of the point values in the table until the entire pattern piece is graded. Hint: The control table can remain open throughout grading. The point numbers of the control table do not represent grade points on a pattern piece.

10. Select *F6>Grading control>Nest* or the keyboard function key *F9* to view the graded nest of the bodice front (Figure 7.4).

Transfer Grading to Another Pattern Piece

1. Digitize a bodice front and back or open the graded bodice front and back file named Graded Bodice Transfer provided on the CD-ROM.

2. Select *F6>Grading modification>Equate* to transfer grade points from the graded bodice front to the ungraded bodice back. Click point 1 of the graded bodice front, and then click point 1 of the ungraded bodice back. Click point 2 of the graded front, and then click point 2 of the ungraded bodice back. Continue matching the same grade rules for the graded front and the ungraded back. Hold the mouse key down on the second point. The space-bar can be used to change direction.

To the Same Pattern Piece

1. To transfer grading to the remaining half of the bodice back, select *F6>Grading modification>Equate.* Click point 2, followed by 11, 3, followed by 10, 4, followed by 9, 5, followed by 8, and 6 followed by 7. The grading will be going in the wrong direction. Note: While many points may be the same on the front and back, it is important to check grade rules, as they are not always the same grade rules.

2. To create a full back, select *F6>Grading modification>XSym*, right-click, and select all the points with grading in the wrong direction. Then left-click one of the points. The grading is now going in the correct direction.

3. Select *F6>Grading control>Nest* or use the keyboard function key *F9* to view the graded nest of the bodice front and back.

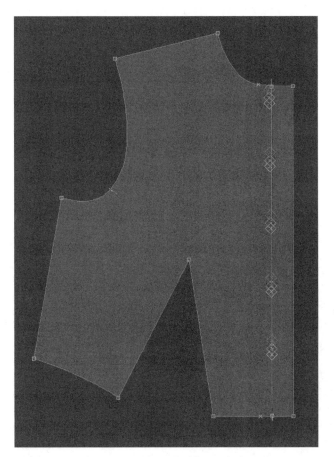

Figure 7.5 Bodice front with graded buttonholes.

Grading Buttonholes

1. Digitize a bodice front with a front extension and add buttonholes to the bodice front as outlined in Chapter 6, or open the bodice file named Bodice with Buttonholes provided on the CD-ROM.

2. Select *F6>Grading control>Control* and grade the top and the bottom buttonholes. Grade the buttons $^4/_{32}''$ in the x-axis and 0 in the y-axis direction.

3. You can grade the buttonholes proportionally with *F6>Grading modification>Pro2Pts* and by right-clicking on all the buttons. Then click the neckline/center front and the hemline/center front, and click any other point. Grade the remaining buttons $^4/_{32}''$ in the x-axis and 0 in the y-axis direction (Figure 7.5). *F6>Grading modification>Equate* can also be used to transfer grades from one point to a second point, such as for buttons.

Control Grading

1. Digitize a bodice front and back and then grade, or open the bodice file named Grading Bodice provided on the CD-ROM.

2. Select *F6>Grading control>Packing*, and click the point to be pack-graded. This effect is for checking side seams or armholes of different angles. Hint: Grading cannot be saved in packing. To display the original grade lines, simply left-click outside the pattern piece.

3. Select *F6>Grading control>Eff. Packing* to save the shape with the desired nest pack.

4. Select *F6>Grading control>Nest* or use the keyboard function key *F9* to view the graded nest of the bodice back.

Exercises

For the grading exercises, follow the procedures outlined under "Grading a New Shape" in this chapter.

1. Open the bodice file named Grading Bodice provided on the CD-ROM. Use the grading points in Figure 7.6 and the incremental amounts in Table 7.3 to grade a bodice back.

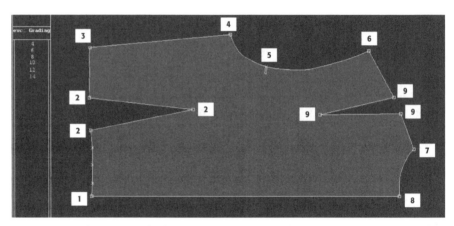

Figure 7.6 Grade points for bodice back.

Table 7.3 Grade for a Basic Bodice Back

Size	Rule 1		Rule 2		Rule 3		Rule 4		Rule 5		Rule 6		Rule 7		Rule 8		Rule 9	
	DX	DY	DX	DY	DX	DY	DX	DY	DX	DY	DX	DY	DX	DY	DX	DY	DX	DY
4	0	0	0	–8	0	–24	–8	–24	0	0	–16	–10	–18	–4	–16	0	–4	–4
6	0	0	0	–4	0	–12	–4	–12	0	0	–8	–6	–10	–2	–8	0	–2	–2
8	0	0	0	0	0	0	0	0	0	0	0	0	0	0	0	0	0	0
10	0	0	0	4	0	12	4	12	0	0	8	6	20	4	8	0	2	2
12	0	0	0	8	0	24	8	24	0	0	8	12	30	8	16	0	4	4
14	0	0	0	12	0	36	12	36	0	0	12	24	40	12	24	0	6	6

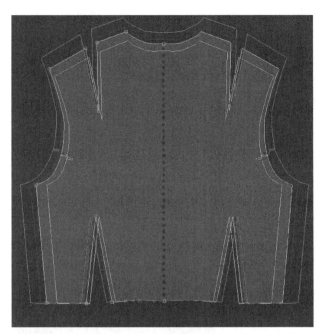

Figure 7.7 Graded nest for bodice back.

2. Select *F6>Grading control>Nest* or the keyboard function key *F9* to view the graded nest of the bodice back (Figure 7.7).

3. Use the grading points in Figure 7.8 and the incremental amounts in Table 7.4 to grade a sleeve.

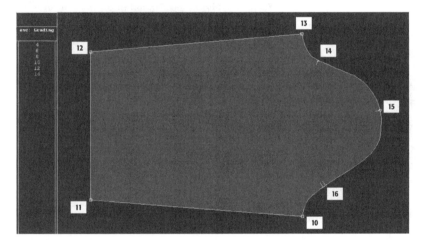

Figure 7.8 Grade points for a sleeve.

Table 7.4 Grade for a Basic Sleeve

Size	Rule 10		Rule 11		Rule 12		Rule 13		Rule 14		Rule 15		Rule 16	
	DX	DY	DX	DY	DX	DY	DX	DY	DX	DY	DX	DY	DX	DY
4	0	12	4	4	4	−4	0	−12	0	−4	−8	0	0	4
6	0	6	2	2	2	−2	0	−6	0	−2	−4	0	0	2
8	0	0	0	0	0	0	0	0	0	0	0	0	0	0
10	0	−6	−2	−2	−2	2	0	6	0	2	4	0	0	−2
12	0	−12	−4	−4	−4	4	0	12	0	4	8	0	0	−4
14	0	−18	−6	−6	−6	6	0	18	0	6	12	0	0	−6

4. Select *F6>Grading control>Nest* or the keyboard function key *F9* to view the graded nest of the sleeve (Figure 7.9).

5. Use the grading points in Figure 7.10 and the incremental amounts in Table 7.5 to grade a two-dart skirt front.

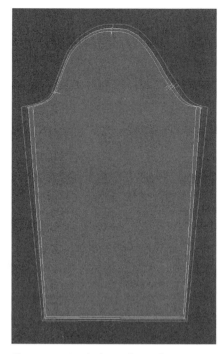

Figure 7.9 Graded nest for a sleeve.

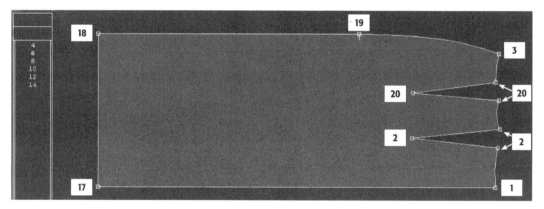

Figure 7.10 Grade points for a skirt front.

Table 7.5 Grade for a Basic Skirt Front and Back

Size	Rule 1		Rule 17		Rule 18		Rule 19		Rule 3		Rule 20		Rule 2		Rule 21		Rule 22	
	DX	DY	DX	DY	DX	DY	DX	DY	DX	DY	DX	DY	DX	DY	DX	DY	DX	DY
4	0	0	24	0	24	−24	16	−24	12	−4	0	−24	12	−4	16	−16	12	−4
6	0	0	12	0	12	−12	8	−12	8	−2	0	−12	8	−2	8	−8	8	−2
8	0	0	0	0	0	0	0	0	0	0	0	0	0	0	0	0	0	0
10	0	0	−12	0	−12	12	−8	12	−8	2	0	12	−8	2	−8	8	−8	2
12	0	0	−24	0	−24	24	−16	24	−12	4	0	24	−12	4	−16	16	−16	4
14	0	0	−36	0	−36	36	−24	36	−16	6	0	36	−16	6	−24	24	−24	6

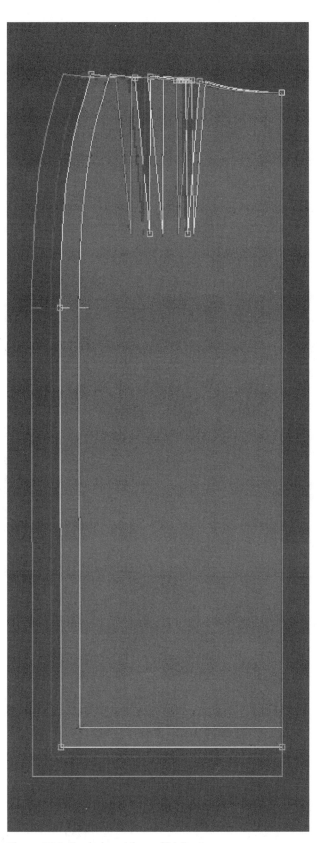

Figure 7.11 Graded nest for a skirt front.

6. Select *F6>Grading control>Nest* or the keyboard function key *F9* to view the graded nest of the skirt front (Figure 7.11).

7. Use the grading points in Figure 7.12 to grade a two-dart skirt back. Table 7.6 is a blank template that you can use to practice grading.

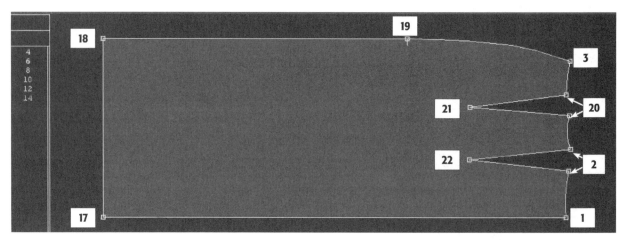

Figure 7.12 Grade points for a skirt back.

Table 7.6 Blank Template for Grading

Size	Rule 00	Rule 00	Rule 00	Rule 00	Rule 00	Rule 00	Rule 00	Rule 00	Rule 00

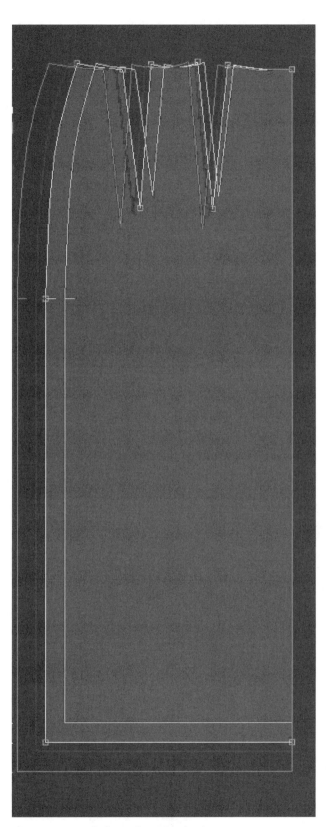

Figure 7.13 Graded nest for a skirt back.

8. Select *F6>Grading control>Nest* or use the keyboard function key *F9* to view the graded nest of the skirt back (Figure 7.13).

Key Terms and Commands

Cartesian graph

Grade point

Grade rule

Graded nest

Grading

F6>Grading Control>Control

F6>Grading Modification>Equate

Dx

Dy

Creating a Variant

8

A variant contains information similar to a cutter's must or direction card. A variant of a model is defined by one or several variations of the model. Variations can include the fabric type or the number of pattern pieces required for a marker. The variant file of a model is the stored pattern pieces for application in **Diamino**, the marker-making program.

In this chapter you will learn about the following:

- Variant Window
- Drop-Down Menus
- Orientation of Pattern Pieces
- Creating a Variant
- Modifying a Saved Variant
- Key Terms and Definitions

Variant Window

The variant window contains a title bar, menu bar, graphic area, and **spreadsheet**. The title bar can be used to move the variant window out of the way when selecting pattern pieces. The menu bar contains drop-down menus with commands specific to creating and modifying variants. Click the name of the menu to open a drop-down menu. Move the cursor down through the drop-down menu to highlight the desired command and then click on the command. The graphic area displays the pattern pieces selected for the variant (Figure 8.1). The spreadsheet or variant table indicates the pattern piece name, number of pieces, and fabric type for the variant. The help line at the bottom of the variant window indicates the required activity for the command currently activated. The Close bar is located at the bottom of the variant window.

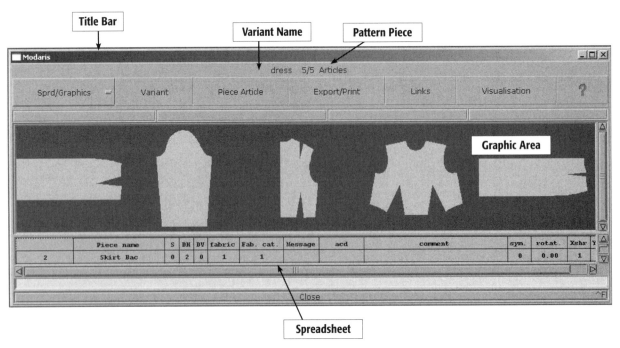

Figure 8.1 Variant window.

Drop-Down Menus

The drop-down menus contain commands specific to creating and modifying variants (Figure 8.2). Spreadsheet, graphics, or both can be displayed in the variant window. The *Variant* menu allows the user to create, copy, or insert pieces in a variant. A new variant can be created without closing the window. *Copy>Variant* displays a variant under a new name. To insert a variant in a current variant, select *Variant>Insert,* and then input the name of the variant.

Piece Article relates to the pattern pieces in the variant. The pattern pieces can be duplicated, deleted, sorted, arranged, or moved. **Duplicate** inserts a pattern piece to the end of the variant table. *Zoom* is used in the variant window to visualize the pattern pieces or graphics. The user can *move* or *rearrange* pieces in order. **Selection** enables the user to make multiple selections with a surrounding box by dragging the mouse around the pattern pieces.

Export>Print is used to save a variant as an ASCII file and print a variant.

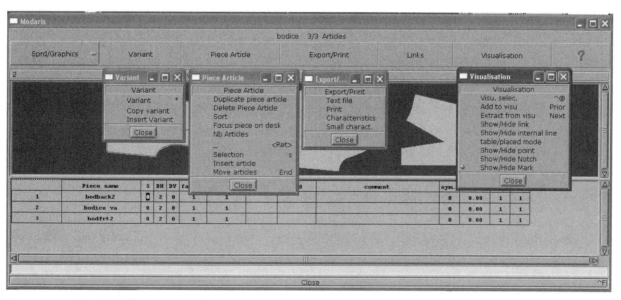

Figure 8.2 Variant drop-down menus.

Visualisation changes what pattern pieces are viewed on-screen. Selected pieces can be removed from view, added to view, or extracted from view. *Visu. selec.,* or selective visualization, allows only the selected pattern pieces to be displayed in the graphic area. *Visu. selec.* can be toggled on or off.

Orientation of the Pattern Pieces

Marker making in Diamino can be more efficient if pattern pieces are oriented in Modaris. In Diamino the fabric length is horizontal on-screen, and fabric width from selvage to selvage is vertically positioned on-screen. You should orient pattern pieces horizontally on the desktop in Modaris prior to creating a variant. Orienting pattern pieces in the horizontal direction or the length of the pattern pieces in the warp direction when placed in Diamino will save you time. If you do not orient the pattern pieces horizontally before creating the variant, then you can rotate the pattern pieces in Diamino when placing them individually in the marker. Hint: Do not have pieces laid both vertically and horizontally if they need to be cut in the same direction.

Creating a Variant

1. Open the bodice file named Bodice no Variant provided on the CD-ROM.

2. Select **F8>Variants>Variant**. The text box prompts you to type in a variant name in the pink bar. Press the Enter key, and the variant window opens.

*Make a new piece!

90° rotation

3. Select **F8>Variants>Create pce article** and click on each pattern piece in the desk to add it to the variant window. The selected pattern pieces automatically appear in the variant window desk area. Hint: If the variant screen is covering a pattern piece, click and drag on the blue title bar at the top of the variant window so the piece underneath it can be viewed.

4. After the required pattern pieces for the garment have been selected, the number and type of each pattern piece needs to be indicated in the spreadsheet (Figure 8.3). The pattern piece name is automatically filled in the first column. *S* represents a single pattern piece in the garment, such as a full back or a pattern piece for an asymmetrical design. When a right and left pattern piece is required in a garment, type "1." DH indicates a right and left in the vertical direction. See Table 8.1 for spreadsheet definitions. Hint: Type "1" in either the *S* or the *DH* column, but not both. A 1 in both columns would indicate three pattern pieces.

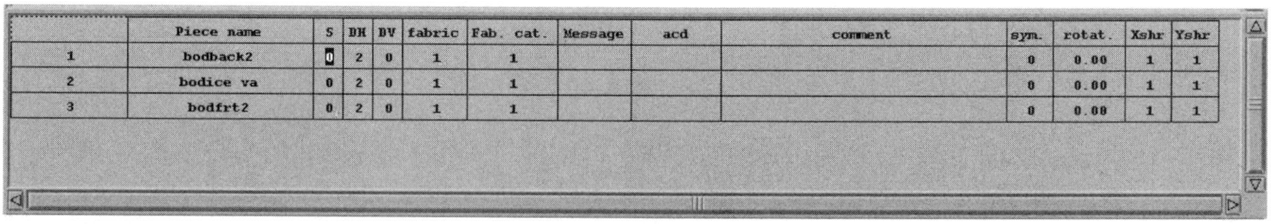

	Piece name	S	DH	DV	fabric	Fab. cat.	Message	acd	comment	sym.	rotat.	Xshr	Yshr
1	bodback2	0	2	0	1	1				0	0.00	1	1
2	bodice va	0	2	0	1	1				0	0.00	1	1
3	bodfrt2	0	2	0	1	1				0	0.00	1	1

Figure 8.3 Variant spreadsheet.

Table 8.1 Variant Spreadsheet Definitions

Piece Name	Name of Basic Image
S	Number of single pattern pieces 0 = None 1 = One
DH	Number of paired pattern pieces 0 = None 1 = One pair A pair is one left and one right pattern piece (placed horizontally).
DV	Number of paired pattern pieces 0 = None 1 = One pair A pair is one top and one bottom pattern piece (placed vertically).
Fabric	Fabric types: self, lining, fusing
Fabric Category	Layers of different colors in graphic display
Message	Additional information
acd	Analytical code
Comment	Additional information
Sym.	Symmetry on the x-axis 0 = No symmetry 1 = x symmetry
Rotate	Applies rotation to a pattern piece related to the grain line
Xshr	Applies shrinkage or enlargement in the X direction of a pattern piece
Yshr	Applies shrinkage or enlargement in the Y direction of a pattern piece

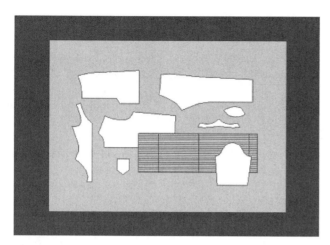

Figure 8.4 Variant sheet.

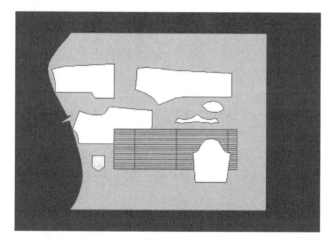

Figure 8.5 Variant sheet with missing model piece.

5. Select *File>Save As* in the Modaris drop-down menu and save your file. Hint: You are saving the same file as previously saved. The variant is part of the Modaris file.

6. Close the variant window. A variant sheet is now visible on the desktop (Figure 8.4). If a variant sheet is cut in half, it indicates that a piece has been deleted from the model but belongs in the variant sheet (Figure 8.5).

Modifying a Saved Variant

Modifying a Variant

1. Select *F8>Variants>Variant* to reopen a previously created variant window.

2. Click the variant sheet on the desk to open the variant.

3. Pieces can be removed from the spreadsheet. Click on the pattern piece name and select *Piece Article>Delete Piece article.*

4. You can also change the number or type of pattern pieces required by typing in the corresponding spreadsheet box. Hint: When selecting pattern pieces, you can minimize the variant window. To open a minimized window, press *Alt + Tab*; when the variant becomes highlighted, release the keys.

Exercises

1. Open the dress file named Dress no Variant provided on the CD-ROM. Create a variant for the file.

2. Open the pant file named Pant no Variant provided on the CD-ROM. Create a variant for the file.

3. Open the bodice file named Knit Dress provided on the CD-ROM. Create a variant for the knit dress.

Key Terms and Commands

Diamino

Duplicate

Export>Print

Piece Article

Selection

Spreadsheet

F8>Variants>Create article

F8>Variants>Variant

Visualisation

Diamino and Marker Making

9

Diamino is the marker-making program that allows markers or pattern pieces to communicate with the printing program. Diamino creates, positions, and sends pattern pieces for plotting all in one window.

A **marker** is a diagram or arrangement of pattern pieces for styles in size(s) that are to be cut at one time. Pattern pieces that fit together allow better fabric utilization and reduce costs of the material. Fabric utilization is affected by factors such as pattern shape and size, interlocking of pattern pieces, fabric selection, and width.

In this chapter you will learn about the following:

- Commands in Completing a Marker
- Opening Diamino
- Diamino Window
- Drop-Down Menus
- Opening a New File
- Opening a Previously Saved Marker
- Preferences Window
- Marker Generalities
- Marker Composition
- Function Area
- Access Paths
- Saving a Marker
- Placing Pattern Pieces
- Creating a Marker
- Exercises
- Key Terms and Commands

Opening Diamino

Diamino can be opened by clicking on the Start button at the bottom left task toolbar and scrolling up to *All Programs>Lectra Systems>Diamino* on the pop-up menu. It can also be opened by double-clicking on the Diamino shortcut icon on the desktop screen. The shortcut icon on the desktop is much faster.

Diamino Window

When Diamino opens, a small pop-up window appears indicating the version of Diamino. Wait and the main working screen opens automatically. The main working screen appears when Diamino is opened (Figure 9.1). The title bar is located across the top of the window. The functions of the title bar are similar to those in Modaris. The buttons at the right of the screen can change the size of the screen, to minimize or enlarge the window. The title bar can also move the screen around. Unlike Modaris, Diamino can be closed by clicking on the red X button at the right of the title bar.

The drop-down menus, with commands specific to the Diamino program, are located across the top of the screen below the title bar. Click the name of the menu to open a drop-down menu. Move the cursor down through the menu to highlight the desired command, and then click the command.

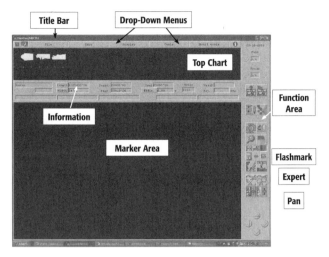

Figure 9.1 Diamino window showing the title bar, drop-down menu, top chart, information, marker area, function area, Flashmark, expert, and pan.

The small black area at the top is the **top chart**. The top chart displays the pattern pieces in the file prior to them being placed in the marker. The top chart displays the size of the pattern pieces, flats of pieces, and the number of right and left pattern pieces are indicated below the flats (Figure 9.2).

The information area below the top chart displays the marker name, length of the marker, width of marker, **marker efficiency**, pattern piece name the cursor is on, and name of the model (Figure 9.3). *Length* indicates the longest length the marker can be made. In Diamino the maximum length is 164 yards. Hint: Pattern pieces can be misplaced along the length. Marker length can be limited by things such as the length of table available. *Used* indicates the actual amount of fabric currently used for the pattern pieces in the **marker area**. *Position* is the placement of an activated pattern piece down the length of marker. *Fabric efficiency* is the percentage of fabric used in a marker— the remaining fabric is waste.

Figure 9.2 Top chart.

torso		Length	112Yd30"00		Posit.	0Yd00"00		Used	0Yd00"00		Scale		VariP		
		Width	54"00		Page	2Yd19"24		Effic.	0,00	%	1/10		Rot.		deg

Figure 9.3 Information area.

The larger black area or desktop is the marker area where the pattern pieces are placed or positioned to create the marker. The **function area** has commands to modify, send pieces to the top, bring pieces to the marker area, and **zoom**. **Flashmark** is an automatic pattern placement to create a marker. *Flashmark* sends all the pattern pieces to the marker area. Note: *Flashmark* does not respect marker constraints. *Pan* scrolls the marker area.

Expert also places pattern pieces like *Flashmark*, but whereas *Flashmark* searches for the best layout in a set period of time, *Expert* continues to lay pattern pieces in different layouts for a set period of time. Both *Expert* and *Flashmark* are useful when a marker is needed quickly for production.

Drop-Down Menus

The drop-down menu options are found along the top of the Diamino screen (Figure 9.4). To open drop-down menus, you click the keywords from *File* to *Motif Tool*.

The *File* menu contains the file-related options, including *New*, *Modify*, *Open*, *Save*, *Save As*, and *Quit* commands found in other computer programs. *New* creates a file never before saved, and *Modify* opens a previously saved file. *New* allows the creation of a new marker by defining the characteristics of the marker.

The *Tools* menu contains the *Generality visu.>Modification* command and opens the generalities and modifications dialog box. The ability to reconfigure the top chart window is also located under *Tools*. The **Preferences** window configures the presentation of the Diamino screen. See the "Preferences Window" section in this chapter for details. *Flashmark* is located under the *Tools* menu and is also found at the function area.

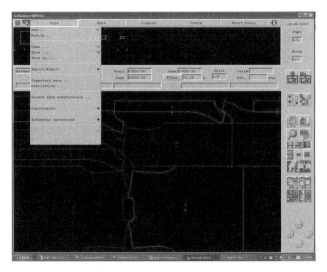

Figure 9.4 Drop-down menu.

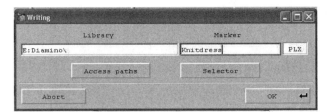

Figure 9.5 Writing a new file.

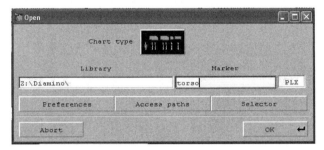

Figure 9.6 Opening a new file.

Opening a New File

The *New* file option is used when no previous file has been saved. When a new file is opened, the text boxes of *Modify the* **Marker Composition** and **Generalities** pop up. The information required to create the file must first be input (see the "Marker Generalities" and the "Marker Composition" sections later in this chapter). The writing text box opens after the marker information has been input. Select *OK* to open the file (Figure 9.5). You can modify the access path or marker name before opening the file. The writing text box automatically closes. Close the Marker Generalities text box, and go to *File>Open* to open the new file (Figure 9.6).

Preferences are the window configuration when a new file is opened. *Access paths* are used to change the library path, and to source the variant and model files. *Selector* is used to find a different file.

Opening a Previously Saved Marker

A previously saved marker can be opened by selecting *Open* or *Modify* under the *File* menu (Figure 9.7). Select *File>Open* when marker generalities or marker composition do not need changing or modification. Select *File>Modification* when marker generalities or marker composition need changing or modification. Once again the library displays the access path where the marker file is to be saved. *Marker* displays the name of the file to be saved. *Abort* exits without opening. *OK* accepts the information and opens the file.

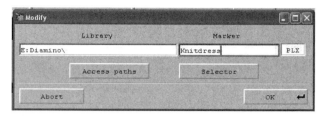

Figure 9.7 Modifying a previously saved file.

Figure 9.8 Preferences window.

Preferences Window

The Preferences window configures the presentation of the Diamino screen (Figure 9.8). Preferences activate with *File>Open*. Preference choices include the presentation of the top chart, pattern pieces in the work area, pattern spacing or screen color, and orientation. The buttons in the *Preferences* dialog box can be toggled on or off.

Top chart can be configured to the user's preference. Pattern pieces can be filled with color or an outline. One of three types of presentations can be selected for the top chart: pattern pieces and number, no chart only a marker, or Flashmark. Below the top chart area are the *Fabric Representation* choices, including folded or unfolded fabric, and plaid or plain fabric. The top chart width, color, and icon positioning can be changed in the marker mode area.

The **B.I. (basic image) representation** in the width section, or marker area, includes options for the labeling of size, grain line, messages, and internal lines display for each pattern piece. Pattern pieces can also be displayed, filled with color, or outlined by their contour by the user toggling the *Filling* button located at the bottom of the *B.I. representation* section in the *Preferences* window. The commands in the *B.I. representation* section of the *Preferences* window can also be found under the *Display* drop-down menu. Preferences also contain marker saving options. A help line is found at the bottom of the *Preferences* dialog box. The *OK* button confirms the selections from the *Preferences* window.

Marker Generalities

In the *Marker generalities* window, the user can establish the fabric criteria for a marker, including fabric width, length, and selvage width (Figures 9.9 and 9.10). The name of the marker is the first line and can be a maximum of nine characters.

The second section of the *Marker Generalities* window includes the fabric width, maximum length, and selvage value. The maximum width of fabric can be 127 inches, and a maximum length of fabric can be 164 yards.

The third section specifies the fabric name that corresponds to the fabric constraint file. Most fabrics do not have constraints. The *Code* field contains additional information regarding the fabric name. The *Type* field refers to the fabric types indicated in the variant window. Hint: Most fabrics are 1. In Diamino there are four choices for fabric layout: open face (faceup), single fold, tubular, or face to face. The fabric type is selected by toggling through the green fabrics. Fabrics can be plain or have motifs such as stripes or plaids. Plain or motif is also a toggle button.

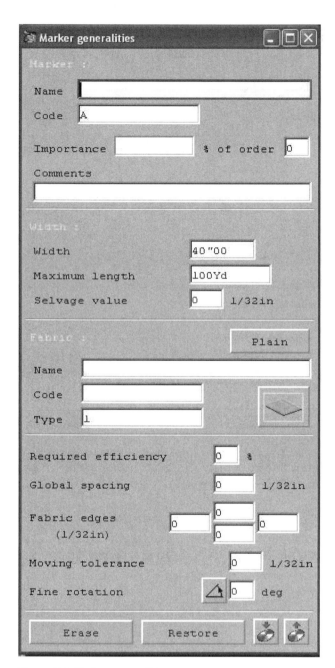

Figure 9.9 Marker generalities.

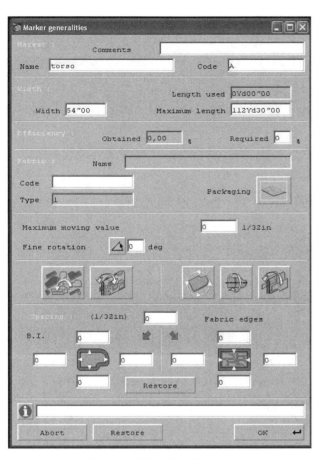

Figure 9.10 Marker generalities drop-down menu.

The bottom section in *Marker generalities* establishes marker efficiency for a marker, fabric edges, and rotation amount. *Efficiency* indicates the amount of fabric that should be used when a pattern is laid. A company usually establishes requirements for the marker. The *Fabric edges* field indicates the distance pattern pieces will be found from the marker edge. *Fine rotation* is the amount a pattern piece can be rotated off grain and still be laid. The maximum allowed in Diamino is 5 degrees. The disc icons located below the *Marker generalities* menu are to save the template or to retrieve a template.

Marker Composition

The *Marker composition* window is used to retrieve the model file and the variant file for the marker (Figure 9.11). The *Model name* and the *Variant name* columns display the files that will be used to create the marker. Double-click the gray box in the *Model name* column to gain access to the access path. Select the model (Figure 9.12). Double-click the gray box under the *Variant name*, and the variant(s) created in the model open in a dialog box (Figure 9.13). Select the variant.

Referring back to the *Marker composition* window shown in Figure 9.11, *Size* indicates the base size. *Dir.* is the direction, which can be either 0 or 1: 0 is the default, and 1 rotates the pattern pieces 180 degrees from the direction they were saved in the variant. Hint: Save the pieces in the direction to be laid in the marker. It saves time. *Group* enables grouping of several sizes or bundles under the same number or placing specific bundles in a group separate from other groups within the same marker. *Qty* is the number of variants needed in the same size. At the top of the composition screen, using the four boxes, the user can duplicate a line, insert a line, delete a line, or delete the entire list. The dark gray line below the model and variant names is a hint line. Once you have input the information, save and then close the *Marker generalities* and *Marker composition* windows.

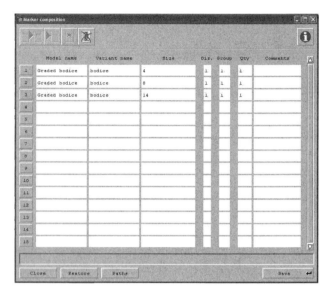

Figure 9.11 Marker composition.

Figure 9.12 Model dialog box.

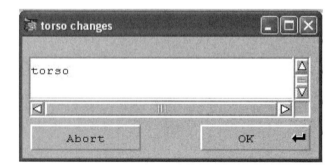

Figure 9.13 Variant dialog box.

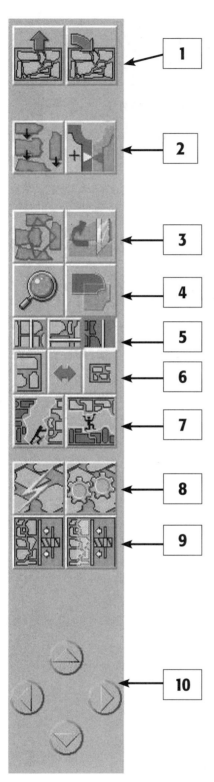

Figure 9.14 Function area.

Function Area

The function area allows modification of the marker (Figure 9.14). Row 1 buttons are to bring down all the pattern pieces from the top chart or to throw all the pattern pieces back up to the top chart. Bringing the pieces down in one step from the top chart will only work if the marker has been previously laid and saved. Row 2 toggles between manual and automatic placement mode when you are selecting a piece from the top area to move to the marker area. The right button allows spacing between the pattern pieces. In Row 3, the **Marriage mode**, pieces can be grouped so they can be moved at one time.

Zoom, in Row 4, allows the user to visualize part of a marker. Select *Zoom* for the marker reduction. A box can also be placed around the area for viewing. The Page Up and Page Down keys can be used to scroll when *Zoom* is activated. Shift + *F7* deactivates *Zoom,* or click the zoom button in the *Marker reduction* dialog box (Figure 9.15). Row 6 toggles between full-size marker and full-view marker. The full-view marker can be modified, unlike full viewing under the *Zoom* command.

The commands in Row 5 are used to indicate a specific length at a specific location on the marker. Row 7 creates gaps in the marker for additional pattern pieces to be placed. The user can split a marker vertically or horizontally to create a gap in Row 7 by clicking between pattern pieces in the marker area after selecting the command. The *Flashmark* option is found in Row 8 and is the same as *Flashmark* under the *Tools* drop-down menu. Row 9 buttons will shake all the pieces together to achieve a higher efficiency. The right button will allow you to select a section to shake (Figure 9.16). Row 10 buttons provide scrolling ability in four different directions to the maximum area of the marker.

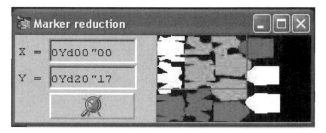

Figure 9.15 Full marker viewing.

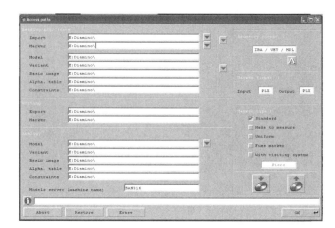

Figure 9.16 Access paths.

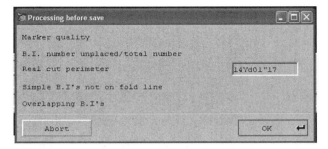

Figure 9.17 Processing before saving.

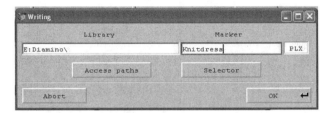

Figure 9.18 Dialog box for saving a new file.

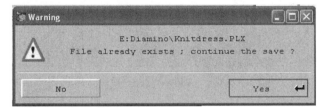

Figure 9.19 A warning appears before continuing with the save.

Access Paths

Access paths are used to locate files when you are opening or saving. For a marker file to open properly in Diamino, it is easier if you save an MDL file down the same access path. Think of two needed files to open a marker. It is not required but makes completing the access path text box easier. When both files are in the same folder, type the path in the first line, followed by a backslash. Then click the blue and red down arrows to fill in the remaining lines. Note: The MDL file can be down a separate path, so if it was saved under a different path, you need to type the file path in the model text line. The help line is found at the bottom of the screen.

Saving a Marker

Before you *Save As*, a dialog box pops open that indicates the length of the marker (Figure 9.17). Select *OK* to proceed with saving. Saving a marker file then requires you to define the library access path and select the marker name (Figure 9.18). *Abort* does not save the most recent work. When *OK* is selected, a warning dialog box opens if a file with the same name has been saved previously (Figure 9.19). The dialog box indicates that a file with the same name already exists and that by selecting *Yes*, the previous file and work will be written over. Selecting *No* will not save the most recent work to the file. Stop and check the access path and file name before saving or the wrong work may be saved.

Placing Pattern Pieces

The keyboard number keys (also called the numeric keypad) are programmed to respond to the functions that place, move, or rotate pattern pieces in the marker area (Figure 9.20). For each command, first press the button and then click the pattern piece in the marker area. Note: Check to make sure number lock (Num Lock) is not on. Press 2 to move the marker area down. The 4 key moves the marker area viewed to the left. Press 5 to rotate pattern pieces 90 degrees. The 6 key moves the marker area viewed to the right. The 7 key sends a single pattern piece from the marker area to the top marker. Press 0 + 7, and all the pattern pieces from the marker area are sent back up to the top chart.

Creating a Marker

1. Open the marker file named Graded Bodice Marker provided on the CD-ROM.

2. Select *Marker generalities*. Rename the marker file.

3. To move pattern pieces from the top chart to the marker area, click a yellow number located below a pattern piece in the top chart. Once the pattern piece is activated, move the cursor to the marker area, and then right-click to place the pattern piece in the marker area (Figure 9.21).

4. After all the pieces are moved from the top chart and placed in the marker area, *Save* the file or *Save As* the file and rename.

Figure 9.20 Keyboard numbers have assigned functions in Diamino.

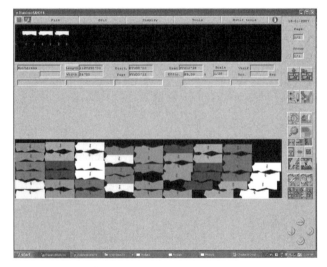

Figure 9.21 Marker.

Exercises

1. Open the files named Marker B and Marker C provided on the CD-ROM. (The file Shirt for B & C allows you to open these marker files.)

2. Make a marker with Marker B using 54″-wide fabric. Repeat Steps 2 to 4 in the "Creating a Marker" section.

3. Make a marker with Marker B using 72″-wide fabric. Repeat Steps 2 to 4 in "Creating a Marker."

4. Compare the fabric utilization of markers 2 and 3.

5. Double the number of garments or sets in the marker on the CD-ROM file named Marker B.

6. Repeat Steps 2 to 4.

Key Terms and Commands

B.I. (basic image) representation

Diamino

Flashmark

Function area

Marker

Marker area

Marker composition

Marker efficiency

Marker generalities

Marriage mode

Preferences

Top chart

Zoom

Appendix A:
Toolbar Function Commands

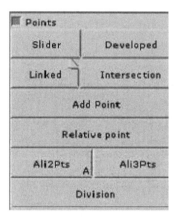

Figure A.1 Points.

The toolbar function menu is located on the right side of the Modaris screen. Keyboard shortcuts are indicated in brackets for corresponding commands.

F1

The F1 function menu contains commands for creating points and lines. Figure A.1 indicates the types of points found on the desktop.

Points (Figure A.1)

F1>Points>Slider allows you to place a point on a line, and because the point belongs to the line, you can slide the point along it. The point keeps proportional position and grading to the original line if changes are made to the line. When you click on an existing line and hold the mouse button down, a point is displayed at the cursor. Release the mouse and the point can be moved between the two endpoints of the line. The point can slide along the line before being permanently placed. Note: The space-bar selects the adjacent line.

F1>Points>Developed (V) places a point at a distance relative to another point on a line. Click a point on a line, then move the cursor to the new position and click to place the new point.

F1>Points>Linked places a point on a line a specific distance from another point. Any changes made to the original point will be made to the linked point. Click on the original point to use as the reference point, move the cursor, and click to place the new point. A dialog box opens and the length between points can be typed.

F1>Points>Intersection (I) generates an intersection point at the intersection of two lines. Click on the line intersection, and the point appears. If two lines are not intersecting, stretch one line to reach and click on the second line; an intersection point appears.

F1>Points>Add Point (Alt-4) adds a characteristic point or a curve point at a relative distance from an original or reference point. Click on a point, then move the cursor to a new position and click to place the new point.

F1>Points>Relative point places a new point in or on the style relative to the first click or anchor point. Click a point on a line or click inside a pattern piece, then move the cursor to the new position and click. The dialog box for relative points contains the same parameters as *F1>Points>Linked.*

F1>Points>Ali2pts (A) is used to orient a pattern piece according to a horizontal or vertical axis. This command is used when pattern pieces are off grain. Click on the hem/center front intersection point and then the hem/side seam intersection point to orient a front pattern piece horizontally.

F1>Points>Ali3pts (Alt + a) aligns a point along a line defined by two reference points. To align the shoulder seam, click the shoulder/armhole intersection point, then the shoulder/neckline intersection point, and lastly the point in the middle of the shoulder seam. Click the two farthest points and then the middle point to align three points.

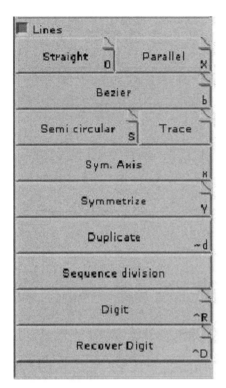

Figure A.2 Lines.

F1>Points>Division adds points automatically at equal intervals when the user clicks two points on a line. A text box appears after the second point is selected. The *division number* is the number of line segments required. The number of line segments is one more than the number of points to be added. In the pink area in the text box, type in the number of line segments and press the Enter key. The dialog box for division contains the same parameters as *F1>Points>Linked.*

Lines (Figure A.2)

F1>Lines>Straight (O) creates a straight line with a beginning point and an endpoint. A straight line has only two points. Click to start a line, move the mouse (cursor) to position until the line is the desired length for the opposite end of the line, and click.

Hold the Ctrl key on the keyboard after the first endpoint is selected. This generates a perfect vertical or horizontal line. Rolling the mouse around the start position in a circular motion allows the line to be created in 45-degree increments. To create an exact line length, use the text box that opens after the first endpoint is selected. Type the length of the line on the x-axis on the *dx* line and the length of the line on the y-axis on the *dy* line.

Associated Parameters

The dialog box for straight lines has three associated parameters. *Maximum constraint* attaches the starting point of the line or object, and the line or objects are connected. This is the default option and is the one most often used. *Magnetism* attaches the line or the object, but the line or object is not connected. With *No constraint,* the starting point and objects are independent and are not attached.

F1>Lines>Parallel (X) creates a line parallel to an existing or reference line. Click the reference line, then move the cursor to the position of the new or parallel line and left-click to place the line. When activated, the *Curve with constraint* option indicates that the parallel lines will be dependent on each other.

F1>Lines>Bezier (b) creates a line that contains both straight and curved segments. Left-click to activate and continue the Bezier line segments. For a curved line segment, hold the Shift key down when left-clicking the segments; release the Shift key to create straight line segments. To undo a line segment and go back to the previous segment, click the right and left mouse buttons simultaneously. Right-click to end the line. The dialog box for Bezier lines contains the same parameters as *F1>Lines>Straight.*

F1>Lines>Semicircular (S) creates a circular line. Left-click to activate, and continue the semicircular line segments. For curved line segments, hold the Shift key down when left-clicking the segments; release the Shift key to create straight line segments. To undo a line segment, click the right and left mouse buttons simultaneously. Right-click to end the command. The curves of the semicircular lines are rounder than the curved lines created by Bezier lines. The dialog box for semicircular contains the same parameters as *F1>Lines>Straight.*

F1>Lines>Trace digitizes lines or internal lines on pattern pieces. Activate the command, and then digitize at the digitizing table.

F1>Lines>Symmetrize is used to create a symmetrical of one or several objects. The dialog box to symmetrize contains the same parameters as *F1>Lines>Parallel.*

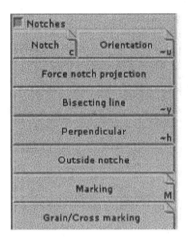

Figure A.3 Notches.

F1>Lines>Duplicate (Alt + d) replicates a flat-pattern object such as a line or the outside line of a pattern piece. Click the object, then place it where required. Hint: A new sheet can be created before obtaining the object required.

F1>Lines>Sequence division divides a contour line into equal segments and places slider points. The lines or spaces between the points are equal to the number in the division text box. The text box for sequence division is the same as for *F1>Division*.

F1>Lines>Digit is used to manually digitize a shape into the computer. Before digitizing, click the dog-ear corner to bring up the dialog box. Select *No Flat Pat.* to eliminate the generation of the flat pattern during digitizing.

F1>Lines>Recover Digit automatically activates when you define the horizontal axis line.

F2

The F2 function menu contains commands for creating and modifying notches and for changing the orientation of pattern pieces, as well as tools for creating geometric shapes.

Notches (Figure A.3)

F2>Notches>Notch (c) places or modifies a notch along a seam line. Click the dog-ear to reveal the dialog box with four different notch types, and select the type of notch required. To change the type of notch, select the notch type and click the previous notch. *F2>Notches>Orientation* (Alt + u) reorients a notch by pivoting the notch end. Zoom in close to select the notch by clicking. The farther the pivot point of the notch, the easier it is to orient the notch. The dialog box for Orientation contains the same parameters as *F1>Lines>Straight.*

F2>Notches>Bisecting divides an angle of two lines and places a notch at an angle created by the two lines.

F2>Notches>Perpendicular orients a notch at 90 degrees to the line to which it is attached. Click the notch, and it automatically orients to the line where it is attached.

F2>Notches>Outside Notch positions existing notches to the outside or the inside of a pattern piece.

F2>Notches>Marking (M) marks a point using a current mark tool. The *Marks* submenu is located in the *Tools* menu.

Orientation (Figure A.4)

F2>Orientation>XSym flips a piece from top to bottom, moving the current sheet in relation to the x-axis. Click the XSym button to change the pattern piece.

F2>Orientation>YSym flips a piece from right to left, moving the current sheet in relation to the y-axis. Click on the pattern piece to activate the change.

F2>Orientation>30>-30>45>-45>90>-90>180 enables rotation at the specific degrees identified. Negative are in the clockwise direction, and positive are in the counter-clockwise direction. Click on the orientation button to activate the change.

F2>Orientation>Rot 2pt rotates the entire pattern piece horizontally between two points, such as endpoints on the center front seam. Click on the pattern piece to activate the change.

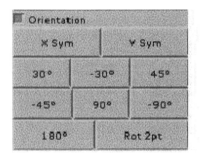

Figure A.4 Orientation.

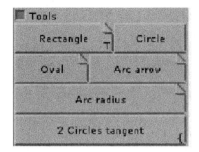

Figure A.5 Tools.

Tools (Figure A.5)

F2>Tools>Rectangle (T) creates a rectangular shape. Click on the desktop, drag the mouse, and click to place the piece. The dialog box for rectangles contains the same parameters as *F1> Lines>Straight*.

F2>Tools>Circle creates a circular shape with five points: two points at the curve's extremity, two points on the circle, and one point at the absolute center of the circle. Click on the desktop, drag the mouse, and click to place the piece. The two points represent the center and outside line of the circle.

F2>Tools>Oval creates an oval shape from two circles. Click on the desktop, drag the mouse, and click to place the oval. The dialog box for ovals contains the same parameters as *F1>Lines>Straight*.

F2>Tools>Arc generates an arc. Click on the desktop, drag the mouse, and click to place. The dialog box for arcs contains the same parameters as *F1>Lines>Straight*.

F2>Tools>Arc Arrow generates an arc from an arrow value. The dialog box for arcs contains the same parameters as *F1>Lines>Straight*. Note: The arrow falls perpendicular in the middle of the arc on the line perpendicular to the arrow.

F2>Tools>Arc Radius generates an arc between two consecutive points from a radius value. The dialog box for semicircular shapes contains the same parameters as *F1>Lines>Straight*.

F2>Tools>Two Circle Tangent creates two circles and the tangent line. Click on the sheet and drag the cursor to create the first circle. Repeat for the second circle. The tangent line will remain when the right mouse button is clicked to end the command.

F3

The F3 function menu contains the deletion button and commands for line and point modification. Pinning or holding pattern pieces in place can also be found under the F3 function menu.

F3>Deletion (Delete) removes points and internal lines from a pattern piece.

Line Modification (Figure A.6)

F3>Line modification>Move (D) can be used to move an entire pattern piece or part of a pattern piece to a new location. Select a pattern piece, and drag to move the entire piece to a new position. Note: *Move* can also be used in combination with *F3>Pins>Pin* to move a selected group of points or part of a pattern piece. After the user has pinned everything, the unpinned area of the pattern can be moved. Points can be pinned. A pinned point appears as a red box.

F3>Line modification>Stretch (Alt + p) repositions or pivots a group of points or a line segment around a central point to create the new pattern shape. Click on the pivot point, and then click the point to be moved, reposition the point, and click. Points may need to be pinned before stretching if an area of a pattern piece is all that requires stretching.

F3>Line modification>Lengthen ($) adjusts the length of a curve line between 2 points. Click on two points and a text box appears. The seam length between the points is indicated in the text box. Type in the new seam length by adding the current length (in the text box) to the additional length desired.

F3>Line modification>Adjust.2 lines is used to adjust a line, either straight or curved on a reference line. Click on the first line, then click on the second line. The first line stretches to the second line.

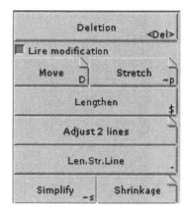

Figure A.6 Line modification.

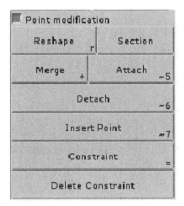

Figure A.7 Point modification.

F3>Line modification>Len.Str.Line (-) extends a line beyond the current pattern piece. Select an endpoint and drag the mouse to length a line. Note: The closer the line is selected near the endpoint, the easier it is to control the movement.

F3>Line modification>Simplify (Alt + s) reduces the number of points or the amount of variation between two points along a curved line, reducing the tolerance in the line for example to smooth. For example, *Simplify* can smooth the shape of a sleeve cap. Click two points along a curved line; a text box opens. The tolerance corresponds to the maximum distance the line can move between two selected points.

F3>Line modification>Shrinkage can enlarge or reduce the size of a piece or a part of a piece with the selection of points. After selecting *Shrinkage*, click on the reference point or the original point. Then input scale value to make the change in the text box.

Point Modification (Figure A.7)

F3>Point modification>Reshape (r) changes the shape of an existing pattern piece. Click a point and move the cursor to the desired position. Then click to set the point in the new position.

F3>Point modification>Section changes a curve point into an endpoint of a line. Click the point to be transformed into an endpoint. Endpoints are usually placed on corners or at the intersections of lines. Endpoints appear as squares.

F3>Point modification>Merge (+) changes an endpoint (square point) into a regular point of a line. Merge is used to connect two line segments. Click the endpoint to be changed. Hint: If an endpoint is no longer needed, merge the endpoint and then delete the point. Note: Bezier curve lines cannot be merged together.

F3>Point modification>Attach (Alt + 5) attaches one point to a second point. Click a point, move the cursor to a second point, and click to create one point. The first clicked point moves to the second point.

F3>Point modification>Detach (Alt + 6) releases a line from a point. Click a point, and the curved line becomes activated. Then click to end the command. Two points are generated from one point.

F3>Point modification>Insert Point (Alt + 7) changes a slider, developed, or intersection point into a characteristic point on a line. Click the point, and it is transformed into a characteristic point.

F3>Point modification>Constraint holds several developed points together.

F3>Point modification>Delete Constraint deletes a constraint on an object. Constraints such as symmetric, parallel, slider, developed, or free objects.

Pins (Figure A.8)

F3>Pins>Pin constrains points on a pattern piece in a fixed place while allowing pattern manipulations, such as *Move* and *Stretch*, to another part of the same pattern piece. Click on points to hold in place.

F3>Pins>Pin graded pts (h) pins graded points on a sheet. Select *Pin graded pts* and the graded points are automatically pinned.

Figure A.8 Pins.

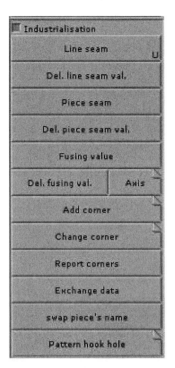

Figure A.9 Industrialisation.

F3>Pins>Pin Characts.Pts pins all characteristic points of a piece on the current sheet. Select pin characteristic points, and the characteristic points are automatically pinned.

F3>Pins>Pin ends (f) pins endpoints of different curves on the current sheet. Select pin ends, and the endpoints are automatically pinned.

F3>Pins>Remove Pin unpins all the points on a pattern piece. Click the *Remove Pin* and the pins are removed automatically.

F4

The F4 functions complete pattern pieces, including commands that create or modify seam allowances.

Industrialisation (Figure A.9)

F4>Industrialisation>Line seam applies a seam allowance to a seam line. When a new pattern piece is derived, the new pattern piece will have seam allowance. Apply a value to one or several seam lines of a pattern to create seam allowances.

F4>Industrialisation>Del.Line seam value enables the user to delete the seam value of one or several lines.

F4>Industrialisation>Piece seam applies a seam allowance to a pattern piece. When a new pattern piece is derived, the new pattern piece will not have seam allowances. Apply beginning and ending seam values to the seams of a pattern piece.

F4>Industrialisation>Del piece seam value deletes the seam value to one or several lines.

F4>Industrialisation>Axis creates a mark as an axis fixed at the ends by a point.

F4>Industrialisation>Add corner applies a corner type to the intersection of the seam allowances.

F4>Industrialisation>Change corner allows the user to assign a corner or modify an existing corner of a pattern piece.

F4>Industrialisation>Exchange data exchanges data between two pattern pieces on the desktop. The information on the title block of a piece is exchanged. Exchange the seam stitching line with the construction line of a pattern piece. The seam allowances will toggle on and off.

F4>Industrialisation>Swap piece's name exchanges the names between two sheets.

F4>Industrialisation>Pattern hook hole places a pattern hook hole inside a piece. The pattern-hole diameter can be adjusted in the dialog box.

Piece (Figure A.10)

F4>Piece>Seam extracts the lines of the pattern as the seam lines.

F4>Piece>Cut creates a separate pattern piece from part of an existing pattern piece. Click inside the pattern piece. When the pattern piece turns green, right-click inside the same pattern piece. A new pattern piece is generated.

F4>Piece>Import Piece imports a piece objects that come from a flat pattern. For example, the user can import notches from one pattern piece to another piece. Only points, lines, and notches can be imported.

F4>Piece>Export Piece removes an object from a pattern piece. Only lines and notches can be removed.

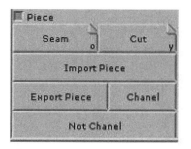

Figure A.10 Piece.

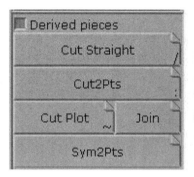

Figure A.11 Derived pieces.

F5

The F5 commands create multiple pattern pieces from a single piece. Dart manipulation and pleat creation is also under the F5 menu.

Derived Pieces (Figure A.11)

F5>Derived pieces>Cut Straight enables cutting a piece into two pieces. The two new pieces are generated. To rotate the straight cut, click the cursor in the pink area beside the word *rotation*. Type in the degree to pivot, or the amount to rotate the line. Then press the Enter key to place the pattern piece. The line on the desktop is now at the desired angle. Two new pattern pieces are generated. Hint: Generally, do not extract with dependency, since a change in one piece will create a change in the other pattern piece.

F5>Derived pieces>Cut2Pts cuts a pattern piece between two points of a pattern piece. Click on two existing points to cut a pattern piece in two pieces. Two new pattern pieces are generated on two new sheets.

F5>Derived pieces>Cut Plot cuts a pattern piece apart along an internal line. Click an existing internal line to cut a pattern piece in two pieces. Two new pattern pieces are generated on two new sheets.

F5>Derived pieces>Join combines two pattern pieces into one new pattern piece. On the first piece, click the endpoint of a line and then click the second endpoint of the same line. The pattern piece is now activated. Move the cursor to the second piece, and click on the two matching endpoints. A new pattern piece is generated.

F5>Derived pieces>Sym2Pts to generate symmetry of a whole or part of a pattern piece. A new pattern piece is generated. Hint: Hold the Shift key down, and the system updates the information on the title block. If the Shift key is not held down, a new sheet will be created. Press the Page Down key to view the new piece.

Folds (Figure A.12)

F5>Folds>Eff.Fold Creation makes it possible to create a fold. The fold line is red, and the background line is green.

F5>Folds>Fold Creation creates a fold line on the original pattern piece.

F5>Folds>Pivoting Dart moves a dart to a new location. To pivot the dart, click the dart apex, then the endpoint of the fold leg of the dart, then the second dart leg endpoint, and then the predetermined point for placement of the new dart. Note: The fold leg of a dart is the leg closest to the front on vertical darts and the lower dart leg on horizontal darts. This folds the darts in the same direction as they are pressed when a garment is constructed. The text box gives you three options for pivoting a dart. The *Ratio* option in the text box is to select the amount of dart to move as a fraction. After typing the amount in the pink area of the text box, press the Enter key. A new pattern piece is created.

F5>Folds>Dart Cap enables the user to create a dart cap or the fold-out end of the dart. A new pattern piece is generated.

F5>Folds>Change Fold Notches enables the user to modify a notch type of a fold, concerning the different folds that will be applied on the fold or dart end created.

Figure A.12 Folds.

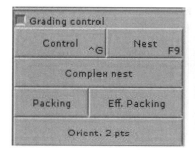

Figure A.13 Grading control.

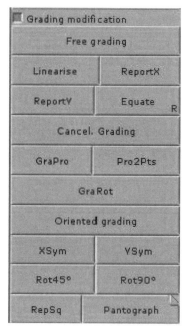

Figure A.14 Grading modification.

F6

The F6 function menu contains the pattern grading commands.

Grading Control (Figure A.13)

F6>Grading control>Control is used to input and modify grade values of specific points for sizes. Once the control button is selected, a text box opens and the grade values can be inputted. The user types in the dx and dy values, while the computer calculates the other values automatically.

F6>Grading control>Nest (F9) displays a graded nest or a set of pattern pieces showing all the sizes in a size range stacked along a common reference line. The graded is displayed on-screen and shows the differences for each successive size.

F6>Grading control>Complex nest displays the nest of selected complex sizes.

F6>Grading control>Packing piles the graded nest on a fixed point.

F6>Grading control>Eff.Packing is used to save the shape with the desired nest pack.

Grading Modification (Figure A.14)

F6>Grading modification>ReportX reports the X movement from one grade point to a second grade point.

F6>Grading modification>ReportY reports the Y movement from one grade point to a second grade point.

F6>Grading modification>Equate allows the transfer of grade points from one point to a second point. The points can be on the same or different pattern pieces. Click point 1 of the graded point, and then click point 1 of a nongraded point.

F6>Grading modification>Cancel.Grading cancels previous graded point, and a 0,0 grade for the x- and y-axis is reported. Click a previously graded point to change the grade rules to 0,0.

F6>Grading modification>GraPro assigns proportional grading at two points, and to all points located on the curve(s) between the two points. This blends the grading between two reference points. Click the two points, holding the mouse down on the second point.

F6>Grading modification>Pro 2pts grades a point or points when the user proportionally right-clicks all the points. Click on the first reference point, and then click on the two reference points. The points take on proportional grading.

F6>Grading modification>XSym is used to flip a grade point from top to bottom or horizontal pivot direction. Select *XSym,* then click on the point to pivot.

F6>Grading modification>YSym is used to flip a grade point from right to left or vertical pivot direction. Select *YSym,* then click on the point to pivot.

F6>Grading modification>RepSq is used to transfer grade rules or a series of points from one pattern piece to a second pattern piece. Click the first point of a graded pattern piece, hold down the spacebar, and click the last point in a series of the graded pattern piece. Then click on point 1 of the nongraded pattern piece and the last point in a series of the nongraded pattern piece.

Figure A.15 Grading rules.

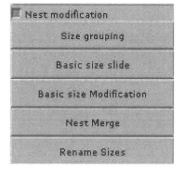

Figure A.16 Evolution system.

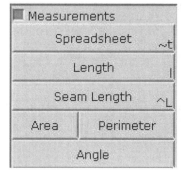

Figure A.17 Nest modification.

F7

Evolution System (Figure A.15)

F7> Evolution System>Imp.EVT Select is used to import a size range for a new style. Click on the model sheet (sheet with the yellow) to bring up the file directory.

F7>Evolution System>Rep.EVT is used to add sizing to all sheets in a file. Choose *Selection>Select all sheets* and click on all the sheets that require sizing in the file. Then select *F7>Evolution System>Rep.EVT* and choose the sizing required.

F7>Evolution System>numeric.EVT converts an alphanumeric EVT into a numeric EVT. Select *F7>Evolution System>numeric.EVT*, then click on the file name of the EVT to be converted.

F8

Nest Modification (Figure A.16)

The F8 menu contains commands for measuring pattern pieces and checking pattern pieces for accuracy.

Measurements (Figure A.17)

F8>Measurements>Spreadsheet opens a table that displays the measurement on one or several pieces.

F8>Measurements>Length (l) measures the length between two points on a straight plane. Click the first point and then hold the cursor at the second point. The distance is displayed on the desktop. Once the second point is clicked, the length text box is no longer visible on-screen.

F8>Measurements>Seam Length (Ctrl L) measures the length between two points or notches on a seam line. Click the first point and then the second point. The distance is displayed on the desktop.

F8>Measurements>Area measures the area of a piece for selected sizes.

F8>Measurements>Perimeter measures the perimeter of a piece, both finished and cut for selected sizes.

F8>Measurements>Angle measures the angle between two lines, for selected sizes.

Assembly (Figure A.18)

F8>Assembly>Stack superimposes two pieces on top of the other and makes the sheets transparent. Select *F8>Assembly> Stack*, click on the first sheet garment point, and then click on the second sheet garment point. The sheets become transparent.

F8>Assembly>Marry (m) temporarily attaches pattern pieces together for checking. *Marry* is used to match two or more pattern pieces or seam allowances to check that pieces are the correct lengths.

F8>Assembly>Move marriages to change the attached position or point of married pattern pieces.

F8>Assembly>Pivot allows two married pieces to be rotated to line pattern pieces or seam allowances. Hint: Hold the Shift key down to flip a pattern piece.

Figure A.18 Measurements.

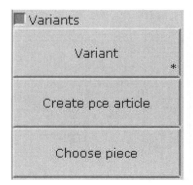

Figure A.19 Dynamics measurements.

F8>Assembly>Walking Pcs. checks the accuracy of pattern pieces. Prior to walking, the pieces must be married. To assemble two pieces together, click the starting point that is attached on the two pieces. Start walking by sliding the cursor along the line to match. Button 3, clicking the right button of the mouse freezes the walking to enable reshaping of the pieces. Click the left to continue walking.

F8>Assembly>Divorce separates married pieces. Click the piece to be separated. Hint: Divorced pieces can be found in the lower right-hand side of the desktop Select *Sheet>Adjust* to resize the sheet of the foundation pattern piece.

Variants (Figure A.19)

F8>Variants>Variant (*) creates a new variant or modifies an existing variant. Select *Variant* and name the variant. To modify a variant, select *F8>Variants>Variant* and then click on the desktop variant.

F8>Variants>Create pce article enables the user to create one or several piece articles in the current variant from a selection of pieces. Articles are added to the end of the table of the current variant.

F8>Variants>Choose Piece enables associating a piece on the desktop (working screen area) to a piece selected in the table of the current variant.

Appendix B:
Pattern Piece Abbreviations

AB	Armhole Back	**CL**	Collar
AF	Armhole Front	**CN**	Center Snap
AH	Armhole	**CP**	Coin Pocket
BA	Back Tab	**CPW**	Coin Pocket Welt
BC	Back Cuff	**CR**	Crotch
BD	Binding	**CS**	Collar Stand
BE	Belt	**CU**	Cuff
BF	Back Facing	**CW**	Center Waistband
BG	Back Gore	**DC**	Drawstring Casing
BH	Back Hem	**EC**	Elastic Casing
BK	Back	**EX**	Extension
BL	Back Loop	**FB**	Front Bottom
BO	Bottom Pocket	**FC**	Front Cuff
BOW	Bow	**FE**	Fly Extension
BP	Back Pocket	**FF**	Front Facing
BR	Bra	**FG**	Front Gore
BT	Back Top	**FH**	Front Hem
BW	Back Waistband	**FL**	Fly
BX	Back Pocket Welt	**FN**	Front Neckband
BY	Back Yoke	**FP**	Front Pocket
CB	Center Back	**FR**	Front
CBG	Center Back Gore	**FS**	Front Sleeve
CBY	Center Back Yoke	**FT**	Front Top
CF	Center Front	**FW**	Front Waistband
CFG	Center Front Gore	**FX**	Front Pocket Welt
CFY	Center Front Yoke	**FY**	Front Yoke
CI	Center Bib	**GD**	Gore Side Back

GF	Gore Side Front	NT	Neck Trim
GO	Godet	PA	Patch
GR	Gore	PE	Placket Extension
GU	Gusset	PF	Pocket Flap
HB	Hood Band	PI	Piping
HD	Hood	PK	Placket
HM	Hem	PR	Pocket Ruffle
HT	Hood Tie	PT	Pocket
IB	Insert Back	PW	Pocket Welt
IF	Insert Front	RB	Right Back
IP	Inside Pocket	RF	Right Front
IT	Inside Top Pocket	RP	Right Pocket
IW	Inside Waistband	RS	Right Side
IX	Inside Pocket Welt	RU	Ruffle
LA	Lapel	SB	Skirt Back
LB	Left Back	SD	Side
LC	Left Cuff	SF	Side Front
LE	Left Extension	SG	Side Gore
LF	Left Front	SI	Side Panel
LFW	Left Front Waistband	SK	Skirt
LN	Left Neck	SKF	Skirt Front
LO	Loop	SL	Sleeve
LP	Left Pocket	SLP	Sleeve Placket
LR	Lower Ruffle	SP	Side Pocket
LS	Left Side	ST	Strap
LT	Left Tab	SW	Side Waistband
LPK	Lower Pocket	SY	Shoulder Yoke
LW	Left Waistband	TA	Tab
LY	Left Back Yoke	TB	Top Back
MB	Middle Back	TE	Template
MK	Middle Back Gore	TI	Tie
MP	Middle Pocket	TR	Top Ruffle
MR	Middle Front	UC	Under Collar
MY	Middle Ruffle	UF	Under Flap
NB	Neck Band	US	Under Skirt
NK	Neck	WB	Waistband
NR	Neck Ruffle	YK	Yoke

Appendix C: Analytical Codes

Pattern Piece	Self	Fuse
Front	FR	FTF
Center front	CF	CFTF
Side front	SF	SFTF
Side	SD	SDF
Right front	RF	RFTF
Left front	LFR	LFTF
Yoke front	YF	YFTF
Upper center front	UCFR	UCFTF
Upper side front	USF	USFTF
Middle front	MF	MFTF
Bottom front	L	BTF
Front facing	FFT	FFTF
Right front facing	RFFT	RFFTF
Left front facing	LFFT	LFFTF
Front armhole facing	FAFFT	FAFFTF

Pattern Piece	Self	Fuse
Back	BK	BKF
Center back	CBK	CBKF
Side back	SBK	SBKF
Right back	RBK	RBKF
Left back	LBK	LBKF
Yoke back	YBK	YBKF
Upper center back	UCBK	UCBKF
Upper side back	USBK	USBKF
Middle back	MBK	MBKF
Lower back	LWBK	LWBKF
Back facing	BF	BFF
Right back facing	RBF	RBFF
Left back facing	LBF	LBFF
Back armhole facing	BAF	BAFF
Skirt	SK	SKF
Front skirt	FSK	FSKF
Right front skirt	RFSK	RFSKF
Left front skirt	LFSK	LFSKF
Back skirt	BSK	BSKF
Right back skirt	RBSK	RBSKF
Left back skirt	LBSK	LBSKF
Overskirt	OSK	OSKF
Top skirt	TSK	TSKF
Middle skirt	MSK	MSKF
Bottom skirt	BSK	BSKF
Middle front skirt	MFSK	MFSKF
Middle back skirt	MBSK	MBSKF

Pattern Piece	Self	Fuse
Pants	PT	PTF
Front pant	FPT	FPTF
Right front pant	RFPT	RFPTF
Left front pant	LFPT	LFPTF
Back pant	BPT	BPTF
Right back pant	RBPT	RBPTF
Left back pant	LBPT	LBPTF
Pocket	PK	PKF
Top pocket	TPK	TPKF
Bottom pocket	BPK	BPKF
Upper breast pocket	UBPK	UBPKF
Upper top pocket	UTPK	UTPKF
Upper bottom pocket	UBPK	UBPKF
Lower pocket	LPK	LPKF
Lower top pocket	LTPK	LTPKF
Lower bottom pocket	LBPK	LBPKF
Pocket band	PKB	PKBF
Pocket facing	PKF	PKFF
Back pocket	BPK	BPKF
Welt	WT	WTF
Upper welt	UWT	UWTF
Lower welt	LWT	LWTF
Flap	FL	FLF
Top flap	TFL	TFLF
Under flap	UFL	UFLF

Pattern Piece	Self	Fuse
Tie	TI	TIF
Tab	TA	TAF
Bias	BIAS	
Bow	BW	BWF
Elastic casing	ELC	
Hood	HD	HDF
Shoulder pad	PAD	
Bra	BRA	BRAF
Crotch	CR	CRF
Gusset	GU	GUF
Ruffle	RU	
Belt	BT	BTF
Right belt	RBT	RBTF
Left belt	LBT	LBTF
Under belt	UBT	UBTF
Waistband	WBD	WBDF

References

Armstrong, H. J. 2005. *Patternmaking for fashion design.* 4th ed. Upper Saddle River, NJ: Prentice Hall.

Handford, J. 2003. *Professional pattern grading.* New York: Fairchild Publications, Inc.

Knowles, L. A. 2005. *The practical guide to patternmaking for fashion designers: Juniors, misses, and women.* New York: Fairchild Publications, Inc.

MacDonald, N. 2002. *Principles of flat pattern design.* 3rd ed. New York: Fairchild Publications, Inc.

Moore, C. L., K. K. Mullet, and M. P. Young. 2000. *Concepts of pattern grading.* New York: Fairchild Publications, Inc.

Price, J., and B. Zamkoff. 1996. *Grading techniques for fashion design.* 2nd.ed. New York: Fairchild Publications, Inc.

Training Guide: Modaris and Files Management. Lectra Systems.

Glossary

A

Access path is the directory structure of the directory or libraries.

Alpha sizes are the size ranges of garments using letters or the alphabet rather than numerical classification, for example S, M, and L.

Apex is the position that marks the tip of the fullest portion of the bust or body bulge; also called the *bust point*.

Armscye is the curved area of the armhole between the mid-armhole, underarm, and side seam intersection.

B

Basic image (BI) is a shape or pattern piece.

Basic image name is the first characters of a garment name. Basic image should reflect the garment to which it belongs.

Blocks are the basic form of garment types; also referred to as foundations, or master patterns—for example, bodices, skirts, pants, and jackets. Blocks generally do not have seam allowances.

Bodice is a garment that covers the female form from the shoulders to the waist.

Bust circle or **pivot circles** are drawn around pivot points and are used to establish new dart tip locations.

Bust point is referred to in flat pattern making as the apex or the pivot point of the bust. Also called the *apex*.

C

Cartesian graph is used to determine *points* on a plane through two numbers, called the x- and y- coordinates. To identify specific points, two *perpendicular* lines mark off on the two axes, and points are identified by their x- and y-coordinates.

Characteristic point is a point located in a line segment.

Collar is a pattern piece added to the neck edge of the bodice designed to frame the face.
>   **Bertha** is a wide, flat collar that extends to cover the shoulders.
>   **Mandarin** is a standing-band collar.
>   **Notched** is a turned-back-lapel collar with a cutout to create the notch.
>   **Peter Pan** is a flat or partial-roll collar with a rounded style line.
>   **Roll line** is the line where the collar turns down.
>   **Sailor** is a flat collar with a square back and V in the front.
>   **Shawl** is a turned-back-lapel collar that has the bodice and the collar cut in one.

Construction lines are the white lines of a pattern on the desktop in Modaris.

D

Dart is a fold of fabric used to shape fabric over a body bulge.
>   **Dart cap** is the shape of the open end of a dart. The dart cap is equivalent to a dart shape at the pattern's end when one is creating a pattern by hand.
>   **Dart leg** is the distance from the pattern seam line to the dart tip.

Desktop is the black area in Modaris where patterns are created and manipulated.

Diamino is the program to create and edit markers.

Digitizing is inputting a pattern piece into the computer. Identifying information, including notches and internal lines, is also inputted.

Directory is the location of files of similar content or type, or with the same extension.

Drill holes are tiny, marked holes that are used to indicate the placement of pockets, dart ends, curved darts, or the end of stitch lines for stitched pleats.

E

Ease is added fullness in width, length, or both to allow for body movement and the desired design effect.

F

File is a saved model or marker.

File extension is the letters automatically attached to a saved file that designates the file type (for example, .mdl).

Flat pattern is a series of points and lines that create a shape. The flat pattern is only the white lines and is not solid blue because does it not belong to a variant.

G

Garment is a list of basic images belonging to a garment and is generated from a variant.

Godet is a triangular piece of fabric set into a garment seam line to add flare.

Graded nest is a set of patterns indicating all the sizes within a size range arranged along a common reference line.

Grade point is the point on a pattern piece that requires a grade rule to create movement or change between the sizes.

Grade rule is the amount of movement required to grade a pattern for a range of sizes. A grade rule is required for each grade point on a pattern piece.

J

JustPrint is a program to plot shapes, variants, and makers.

L

Library is a directory for storing files, for example markers, garments, shapes, and alpha tables.

M

Marker is a layout of pattern pieces of a style for a cutting layout.

Marker composition window is used to retrieve a model file and variant file for a marker in Diamino.

Marker generalities window is used to establish the fabric criteria for a marker in Diamino.

Midriff is the fitted part of a garment, usually below the bust to the waist.

Modaris is a computer-aided pattern-making program that is used to enter blocks or foundation pattern pieces into the system through the use of a digitizer.

Model is a file created in Modaris that holds all the pattern pieces, including flat pattern pieces and variants that belong to one style.

N

Notches are shapes "cut" into the seam allowance on a pattern piece to match pieces together.

Numeric sizes are the size ranges of garments using numbers rather than the alphabetical classification, for example, 4, 6, 8, 10, and 12.

O

On the fold refers to the placement of a pattern piece that is to be cut with the fabric folded over on itself.

P

Page Down is the key on the keyboard that allows the user to view the next sheet in order on the desktop. One sheet at a time is viewed.

Page Up is the key on the keyboard that allows the user to view the previous sheet in order on the desktop. One sheet at a time is viewed.

Path is the location for saved files consisting of the drive name, Modaris or Diamino folder, and additional user files created, for example, C:\Lectra\Modaris\Data\bodice.mdl.

Pattern drafting is the process of creating a pattern on the desktop or on-screen in Modaris.

Pattern grading is the increasing or decreasing of the dimension of a master pattern (pieces) into a range of production pattern (pieces) within a size range. Grade changes are based on systematic changes to/of a base pattern using grade rules.

Pattern making is the process of creating a pattern. Traditionally, patterns are created by hand, using drafting, draping, or flat pattern techniques.

Pattern orientation is the direction that a pattern piece is laid on the digitizer or viewed on-screen in Modaris.

Peripherals are the hardware added to the host or hard drive of a computer to expand the computer's abilities, for example, print screen, digit table, and scanner.

Piece article is referenced to a pattern piece that belongs to a model.

Pivot circle is the circle around a pivot point used to establish a new dart end or tip location.

Plotting is the printing of pattern pieces.

S

Shape is one pattern piece.

Sheet holds the shape and all of its information in Modaris.

Sleeve capline is the line that separates the upper portion of a sleeve from the arm portion of a sleeve at the bicep.

Spreadsheet is a chart that is filled with information relating to the specific model, including pattern piece names, number of pieces to cut, and fabric information.

T

Title block is the yellow field surrounding the sheet that holds the shapes and information regarding the pattern (see Chapter 3).

Toolbar menu commands are used to create, modify, or grade pattern pieces.

V

Validate is the acceptance of a function or command with the click of the right mouse.

Variant holds the list of shapes that creates one style variation and belongs to one model.

One model can have one or several variants. The variant specifies each shape, fabric type, and number of pieces to be cut, as well as other cutting information. A variant in the Modaris system is the apparel industry's version of a "cutter's must."

Vigiprint is a program to plot shapes, variants, and makers.

W

Warp direction is the length direction of fabric.

X

X-axis is the horizontal axis in a Cartesian graph.

Y

Y-axis is the vertical axis in a Cartesian graph.

Yoke is the fitted portion of a garment across the shoulders (at front or back) or the fitted top of a skirt.

Z

Zoom In tool is found at the bottom of the function tools menu and is used to move closer to an image and view a smaller portion.

Zoom Out tool is found at the bottom of the function tools menu and is used to move farther from an image and view a larger portion.

Zoom to Fit tool is found at the bottom of the function tools menu and is used to fit an entire image on the screen or desktop.

Index